SANTANDER

TRAVEL GUIDE

2024

A Comprehensive Guide to Urbino's Hidden

Gems, Top Attractions, Stellar Accommodations,

Museums, Rich Culture and Vibrant Nightlife

WILLIAMS D. MOORE

Copyright © 2024, WILLIAMS D. MOORE

TABLE OF CONTENTS

INTRODUCTION

CHAPTER ONE

- ❖ Overview of Santander

- ❖ Purpose of the Travel Guide

CHAPTER TWO

- ❖ Getting Started

- ❖ Planning Your Trip

- ❖ Travel Essentials

- ❖ Local Customs and Etiquette

CHAPTER THREE

- ❖ Santander's Hidden Gems

- ❖ Off-the-Beaten-Path

- ❖ Charming Cafés and Boutique Shops

- ❖ Scenic Walking Trails

CHAPTER FOUR

- ❖ Santander's Top Attractions

- ❖ Historic Landmarks

- ❖ Natural Wonders

- ❖ Adventure Palette

CHAPTER FIVE

- ❖ Stellar Accommodations

- ❖ Luxury Hotels

- ❖ Bed and Breakfast Charm

- ❖ Budget-Friendly Gems

CHAPTER SIX

- ❖ Museums and Experiences

- ❖ Art Galleries

- ❖ Historical Museums

- ❖ Interactive Cultural Events

CHAPTER SEVEN

❖ Rich Culture

❖ Local Cuisine and Culinary Delights

❖ Festivals and celebrations

❖ Traditional Arts and Crafts

CHAPTER EIGHT

❖ Vibrant Nightlife

❖ Trendy Bars and Pubs

❖ Live Music Venues

❖ Night-time Entertainment

CHAPTER NINE

❖ Practical Tips for Travellers

❖ Transportation Guide

❖ Safety and Security

❖ Language Symphony

CHAPTER TEN

❖ Santander in Every Season

❖ Spring

❖ Summer

❖ Autumn

❖ Winter

CHAPTER ELEVEN

❖ Glossary of Local Terms

INTRODUCTION

Welcome to the enchanting world of Santander, where every cobblestone whispers tales of history and each panoramic view is a canvas painted with the vibrant hues of rich culture. This comprehensive handbook is your passport to discovering the hidden gems, top attractions, stellar accommodations, museums, and the pulsating nightlife that makes Santander a must-visit destination.

In the following pages, we invite you to embark on a journey that transcends the ordinary, guiding you through the heart of Santander's essence. Whether you're a curious traveller planning your first visit or a seasoned explorer seeking new facets of this charming city, this guide is tailored to unveil the wonders that await you.

Santander is not just a destination; it's an immersive experience. We delve beyond the surface, revealing the soul of this coastal gem nestled between the mountains and the sea. From the cobblestone streets of historic neighbourhoods to the vibrant rhythm of its nightlife, Santander beckons you to explore, savour, and embrace the captivating spirit that defines this unique corner of the world.

So, fasten your seatbelt and turn the page. Let the journey begin, an odyssey through Santander's hidden treasures, cultural tapestry, and the pulsating heartbeat that resonates through its streets. The adventure awaits, and Santander is ready to captivate your senses and leave an indelible mark on your travel memories.

CHAPTER ONE

Overview of Santander

Nestled gracefully on the northern coast of Spain, Santander stands as a testament to the seamless blend of natural beauty and historical charm. This coastal jewel, cradled between the Bay of Biscay and the Cantabrian Mountains, unfolds a captivating tapestry of landscapes that range from sun-kissed beaches to lush green hills.

Santander, the capital of the Cantabria region, exudes an inviting aura, drawing travellers into its embrace with open arms. The city's history breathes life into its architecture, where ancient cathedrals and palaces whisper stories of bygone eras. Yet, amidst this rich tapestry of tradition, Santander is also a city in constant evolution, a vibrant hub where modernity gracefully coexists with its storied past.

The Bay of Santander, with its sweeping crescent shoreline, serves as a natural amphitheatre to the city's maritime soul. Watch as sailboats dance on the shimmering waters, painting a picturesque backdrop to the bustling cityscape. From the emblematic Magdalena Palace to the lively streets of El Sardinero, every corner of Santander invites exploration and discovery.

As you traverse the city's meandering streets, you'll find a culinary scene that mirrors the diversity of its landscapes. Savoury seafood delicacies, tantalising pintxos, and robust local wines await gastronomic enthusiasts, promising a journey for the taste buds as well.

In this enchanting city, time seems to slow down, allowing travellers to immerse themselves in the unhurried rhythm of life. Santander is not merely a destination; it's a living canvas where each sunrise paints a new story, and each sunset whispers the promises of another day of adventure.

Join us as we unravel the layers of Santander, a city that captivates the senses, leaving an indelible mark on all who are fortunate enough to explore its shores.

Purpose of the Travel Guide

This travel guide is more than just a compilation of facts and figures; it's a compass guiding you through the heart and soul of Santander. Our purpose is to transform your visit into an unforgettable journey, ensuring that every step you take in this coastal haven is enriched with discovery, wonder, and cultural immersion.

1. Unveiling Hidden Treasures

Beyond the well-trodden paths, we aim to illuminate the hidden gems that define Santander's character. From tucked-away cafés with stories to tell to scenic trails that lead to panoramic vistas, this guide is your key to unlocking the city's best-kept secrets.

2. Navigating Top Attractions

Whether you're an avid history buff, a nature enthusiast, or an adventure seeker, Santander has something for everyone. We meticulously curate insights into the city's top attractions, ensuring you make the most of your time exploring historic landmarks, natural wonders, and thrilling activities.

3. Crafting Cultural Experiences

Santander is not merely a destination; it's an immersive cultural journey. This guide is designed to immerse you in the vibrant tapestry of Santander's rich cultural scene. From art galleries and museums to local festivals and traditional crafts, you'll discover the city's beating cultural heart.

4. Nurturing Practical Travel

Travelling is not just about the destination but the journey itself. Our guide provides practical tips for travellers, helping you navigate transportation, ensuring your safety, and bridging any language gaps. We want your experience in Santander to be seamless, allowing you to focus on creating lasting memories.

5. Personalising Your Santander Experience

Santander is different things to different people. Whether you're seeking a romantic escape, a family adventure, or a solo exploration, this guide adapts to your preferences. Our goal is to empower you to tailor your Santander experience to match your unique travel aspirations.

6. Seasonal Exploration

Santander's beauty evolves with the changing seasons. In these pages, we guide you through the city's different faces, from the blossoms of spring to the cosy charm of winter. Each season offers a distinct ambiance, allowing you to choose the perfect time to savour Santander's diverse offerings.

7. Local Insights and Authenticity

Beyond the written words, we bring you closer to Santander through local insights and interviews. Engage with the stories of residents, gain insider tips, and immerse yourself in the authenticity that defines the city. This guide strives to connect you with the heartbeat of Santander, ensuring a genuine and enriching experience.

8. Practical Tools for Exploration

From detailed maps for seamless navigation to a curated glossary of local terms, this guide is equipped with practical tools to enhance your exploration. We want you to feel empowered and well-prepared, allowing you to embrace the spontaneity of travel without sacrificing comfort or convenience.

9. Acknowledging Collaboration

Santander is a collective masterpiece shaped by its community. In the spirit of gratitude, we acknowledge the contributions of locals, collaborators, and experts who have shared their knowledge and passion. This guide is a celebration of the collaborative effort to showcase Santander in all its glory.

10. Index and Beyond

To ensure easy reference, an index is provided for quick navigation. Beyond your journey's end, we offer resources for further exploration, allowing Santander to linger in your memories long after you've bid the city farewell.

As you embark on this adventure through the pages of our guide, may the spirit of Santander captivate your senses, and may each moment become a cherished chapter in your travel story. Here's to unlocking the treasures of Santander – a city that invites you not just to visit but to truly experience its magic.

CHAPTER TWO

Getting Started

Embarking on your Santander adventure is like opening the door to a world of endless possibilities. As you stand on the threshold of discovery, this section serves as your compass, guiding you through the essential steps to ensure a seamless and enchanting journey.

1. Planning Your Santander Sojourn

Dive into the heart of Santander by crafting a thoughtful itinerary. Uncover the diverse neighbourhoods, map out your must-visit attractions, and leave room for serendipitous discoveries along the way. Let your imagination roam, and create a roadmap for a journey uniquely tailored to your preferences.

2. Travel Essentials Unveiled

Before you set foot on Santander's shores, equip yourself with the knowledge of travel essentials. From weather considerations to local currency nuances, this guide ensures you are well-prepared, leaving you free to relish every moment without the worry of logistical hiccups.

3. Navigating Local Customs and Etiquette

Santander's charm extends beyond its landmarks; it lies in the warmth of its people. Gain insights into local customs and etiquette, allowing you to engage with the community authentically. Whether savouring traditional cuisine or participating in local celebrations, understanding these cultural nuances enhances your Santander experience.

As you immerse yourself in the preparations, envision the vibrant scenes, the tantalising aromas, and the echoes of laughter that await. Your journey is not just a passage through space but a seamless fusion with the spirit of Santander. So, let the anticipation build, and let each preparation be a step towards creating memories that will last a lifetime. Your Santander adventure begins now.

Planning Your Trip

Crafting Your Santander Sojourn

Embarking on a journey to Santander is not just about travel; it's a canvas awaiting your unique brushstrokes. Planning your trip is the first stroke, the inception of an adventure that promises to be as diverse as the landscapes that define this coastal gem.

1. Unravelling the City's Tapestry

Begin your journey by delving into the intricacies of Santander's neighbourhoods. Each has its own story to tell, from the historic charm of the Old Town to the modern allure of El Sardinero. Unravel the city's tapestry, allowing your curiosity to guide you through the cobbled streets and vibrant districts.

2. Mapping Out Must-Visit Attractions

Santander boasts a treasure trove of attractions waiting to be discovered. Craft a list of must-visit landmarks, from the regal Magdalena Palace to the awe-inspiring Picos de Europa. Let your interests dictate your choices, ensuring your itinerary reflects the diverse facets of Santander's allure.

3. Balancing Time for Serendipity

While planning is essential, leave room for the unexpected. Santander's charm often lies in serendipitous discoveries – a hidden café, an impromptu street performance, or an unexpected viewpoint. Build flexibility into your schedule, allowing the city to surprise and delight you with moments you never anticipated.

4. Savouring Culinary Exploration

Santander's culinary scene is a feast for the senses. Research local eateries, traditional dishes, and hidden gems that promise gastronomic delights. Whether indulging in a leisurely meal at a seaside restaurant or savouring pintxos in a cosy tavern, let the city's flavours be an integral part of your travel experience.

5. Embracing Cultural Calendar

Santander pulsates with cultural events throughout the year. Check the local calendar for festivals, art exhibitions, and performances aligning with your visit. Immerse yourself in the city's cultural vibrancy, connecting with its artistic and celebratory spirit.

As you plan, envision the unique narrative your journey will weave. Santander is not merely a destination; it's an immersive story waiting to be written. Let your planning be the prologue, setting the stage for a travel tale that unfolds with every step you take in this captivating city by the sea.

6. Tailoring Activities to Your Interests

Santander offers a kaleidoscope of activities catering to diverse interests. Whether you're an art enthusiast, nature lover, or history buff, tailor your itinerary to align with your passions. From exploring art galleries to hiking picturesque trails, let Santander be a reflection of your personal travel preferences.

7. Anticipating Seasonal Nuances

Consider the seasonal nuances that shape Santander's character. Spring blooms, summer beach vibes, autumn's golden hues, and winter's cosy charm, each season brings a unique ambiance. Anticipate the weather and cultural nuances to enhance your experience, ensuring your visit aligns with the atmosphere you desire.

8. Seizing Photographic Opportunities

Santander is a visual masterpiece waiting to be captured. Identify iconic landmarks, scenic viewpoints, and charming corners ideal for photography. Let your lens tell the story of your journey, capturing not just moments but the essence of Santander's beauty.

9. Exploring Day and Night

Santander transforms as day turns to night. Plan to explore the city during both daylight and evening hours. While the sun bathers landmarks in a golden glow, the city's nightlife adds a dynamic energy. Embrace the contrast, ensuring your itinerary accommodates the full spectrum of Santander's allure.

10. Incorporating Local Recommendations:

Seek out local recommendations and tips from residents or fellow travellers who have explored Santander. Embrace the wisdom of those who know the city intimately, enhancing your itinerary with insider insights that may lead to hidden gems and authentic experiences.

As you fine-tune your Santander adventure, remember that the planning process is not just a logistical exercise; it's an opportunity to anticipate the magic that awaits. Your journey is a canvas, and the brush is in your hands. May every stroke be a step closer to a Santander experience that transcends expectations, weaving memories that linger long after you bid this enchanting city farewell.

Travel Essentials

Embracing Santander: Your Travel Essentials

Preparing for your Santander escapade is not just about packing bags; it's a ritual of readiness, an embrace of the essentials that will enhance your journey through this coastal masterpiece. As you embark on this adventure, consider these travel essentials as your companions, ensuring a seamless and enriched experience.

1. Dressing for Santander's Rhythms

Santander's climate dances to its own rhythm, so pack accordingly. From the gentle sea breeze to occasional rain showers, be prepared for varied weather. A mix of comfortable layers, a sturdy pair of walking shoes, and a light waterproof jacket will equip you for Santander's atmospheric surprises.

2. Currency and Cash Wisdom

Venture into Santander's markets and local establishments armed with local currency. While credit cards are widely accepted, having cash on hand is practical, especially in smaller shops and traditional eateries. Immerse yourself in the city's culture by engaging in local transactions with ease.

3. Language Essentials

While English is understood in many tourist spots, embracing a few basic Spanish phrases will enhance your interactions and endear you to the locals. A pocket-sized Spanish phrasebook or a language app can be valuable companions, allowing you to navigate conversations with confidence.

4. Powering Your Adventures

Ensure your devices stay charged to capture every Santander moment. A universal adapter will be your ally, allowing you to plug in and recharge your camera, phone, and other gadgets. Be ready to document the visual poetry that unfolds as you explore the city.

5. Navigational Wisdom

Santander's winding streets are a joy to explore, but a map or navigation app ensures you never lose your way. Arm yourself with a city map or a reliable navigation app to navigate effortlessly through the cobblestone alleys and discover hidden gems tucked away in the corners.

6. A Taste of Santander

Immerse yourself in Santander's culinary delights by carrying a reusable water bottle and a sturdy tote bag. Stay hydrated with water from the city's fountains and be eco-conscious by reducing single-use plastic. The tote bag comes in handy for impromptu purchases in local markets.

7. Weather-Ready Accessories

Santander's weather can be whimsical, so be prepared with accessories that cater to unexpected changes. A stylish sun hat for warm afternoons, a compact umbrella for sudden rain showers, and a pair of sunglasses will add flair to your ensemble while keeping you comfortable.

8. Documenting Memories

A travel journal or a digital notepad ensures you capture the nuances of your Santander experience. From the taste of local delicacies to chance encounters with locals, these essentials become the canvas on which you paint the narrative of your journey.

As you gather these travel essentials, envision them not just as items in your suitcase but as companions on your Santander odyssey. Each item has a purpose, adding to the symphony of experiences that await you in this coastal city. So, pack with intention, embrace the essentials, and let Santander's magic unfold.

Local Customs and Etiquette

Embracing Santander's Heart: Local Customs and Etiquette

In the vibrant tapestry of Santander, understanding and embracing local customs and etiquette is the key to unlocking the city's true spirit. Beyond the architectural wonders and scenic landscapes, it is the warmth of the people that defines the soul of Santander. As you navigate the charming streets and engage with the locals, consider these cultural nuances to enhance your connection with this coastal gem.

1. Greetings with Genuine Warmth

Santanderinos are known for their warmth and friendliness. When meeting with someone, a friendly "Hola" (hello) accompanied by a genuine smile goes a long way. Handshakes are common in formal situations, while close friends and family may exchange kisses on both cheeks. Embrace these gestures, allowing the sincerity of your greetings to mirror the city's hospitality.

2. Embracing the Siesta Tradition

Santander follows the Spanish tradition of siesta, a midday break where many businesses close for a few hours. Embrace this cultural practice by slowing down during this time. Enjoy a leisurely lunch, explore quieter neighbourhoods, and savour the unhurried rhythm that defines Santander's afternoons.

3. Politeness in Public Spaces

Courtesy in public spaces is highly valued in Santander. Maintain a respectful volume when conversing, especially in restaurants and public transport. Be mindful of personal space, and practise patience in queues. These small gestures contribute to the harmonious coexistence that characterises life in this coastal city.

4. Savouring Culinary Moments

Dining in Santander is not just a meal; it's a social and cultural experience. When dining out, linger over your meal, savouring the flavours and enjoying the company of those around you. It is common to engage in lively conversations, appreciating the art of culinary exploration as a shared joy.

5. Respect for Local Customs

Santander has a rich cultural tapestry, and locals take pride in their traditions. Respect local customs, whether it's participating in festivals, observing religious ceremonies, or appreciating the arts. Immerse yourself in the city's heritage, fostering a deeper connection with the community.

6. Tipping with Appreciation

Tipping is a customary practice in Santander, and it reflects appreciation for good service. While it's not mandatory, rounding up the bill or leaving a small percentage is a thoughtful gesture. Your generosity acknowledges the dedication of those who contribute to making your Santander experience memorable.

7. Learning a Few Basic Phrases

While English is widely understood, locals appreciate visitors who make an effort to speak Spanish. Learning a few basic phrases not only enhances your communication but also demonstrates a genuine interest in the local culture. Simple expressions like "gracias" (thank you) and "porfavor" (please) go a long way in fostering positive interactions.

8. Adapting to Relaxed Pacing

Life in Santander moves at a more relaxed pace, inviting you to embrace the unhurried moments. Adapt to this rhythm by allowing time for leisurely exploration, enjoying extended meals, and relishing the spontaneous beauty of the city. In Santander, the journey is as important as the destination.

9. Celebrating Local Festivals

Santander's calendar is dotted with vibrant festivals, each offering a unique glimpse into the city's cultural richness. Participate in local celebrations, whether it's the lively Semana Grande or a traditional neighbourhood festival. Engaging in these festivities allows you to witness the joy and camaraderie that define Santander's community spirit.

10. Cherishing Family and Community

Family holds a special place in Santander's culture, and the importance of community is deeply ingrained. If invited into a local home, it is customary to bring a small gift as a gesture of appreciation. Embrace the opportunity to share stories and experiences, fostering connections that extend beyond the tourist experience.

11. Admiring Art and Craftsmanship

Santander's artistic heritage is woven into its daily life. When exploring local markets or artisan shops, take time to appreciate the craftsmanship of handmade goods. Whether it's a piece of traditional pottery or a locally crafted souvenir, acquiring these treasures allows you to carry a piece of Santander's artistic spirit with you.

12. Gracious Farewell Gestures

As your Santander journey concludes, consider expressing your gratitude with a heartfelt farewell. Whether it's a simple "adiós" or a sincere thank-you to those who made your stay memorable, these parting gestures contribute to the positive connections forged during your time in Santander.

13. Embracing the Spirit of Generosity

Santanderinos are known for their generous and inclusive nature. If invited to join locals in a social activity or celebration, accept the invitation with openness. These shared experiences allow you to delve deeper into the cultural fabric of Santander, creating memories that extend beyond the typical tourist encounter.

14. Environmental Respect

Santander's natural beauty is a treasure to be cherished. Practise environmental respect by disposing of waste responsibly and appreciating the delicate ecosystems that surround the city. Embrace eco-friendly practices, such as using reusable bags and water bottles, contributing to the preservation of Santander's pristine landscapes.

As you weave through the cultural nuances of Santander, remember that it's not just about following customs but about embracing the heart and soul of the city. Santander's warmth and authenticity await those who approach with an open mind and a genuine appreciation for its traditions. May your journey be enriched by these cultural connections, leaving you with memories that echo the spirit of Santander for years to come.

CHAPTER THREE

Santander's Hidden Gems

Unveiling Santander's Hidden Gems: A Treasure Hunt for the Curious

Santander, like a well-kept secret, reveals its true magic in the hidden corners waiting to be explored. Beyond the well-known landmarks, these hidden gems are the city's whispered stories, beckoning the curious traveller to venture off the beaten path and uncover Santander's most enchanting secrets.

1. Mystical Old Town Alleys

Lose yourself in the enchanting labyrinth of alleys within the Old Town. Cobbled streets adorned with vibrant flowers lead to hidden squares where time seems to stand still. Discover tucked-away cafes, artisan workshops, and boutiques, each exuding an old-world charm that immerses you in Santander's rich history.

2. Paseo **de Pereda's Evening Glow**

Experience the magic of Paseo de Pereda as the sun dips below the horizon. Stroll along the waterfront promenade, and witness the gentle transition from daylight to the soft glow of evening lights. This hidden gem offers a serene setting, where the rhythm of the sea harmonises with the city's evening whispers.

3. **Mercado de la Esperanza's Culinary Kaleidoscope**

Step into the Mercado de la Esperanza, a bustling market that awakens the senses. Amidst the stalls laden with fresh produce and artisanal delights, discover the heart of Santander's culinary scene. Engage with vendors, savour local flavours, and immerse yourself in a gastronomic treasure trove that remains off the tourist radar.

4. Jardines de Piquío's Seaside Serenity

Escape to the Jardines de Piquío, a serene oasis nestled along the coastline. These picturesque gardens offer a tranquil retreat, inviting you to unwind amidst lush greenery with panoramic views of the sea. It's a hidden gem that encapsulates Santander's blend of nature and urban beauty.

5. Iglesia de la Anunciación's Architectural Elegance

Venture beyond the well-known churches to discover the Iglesia de la Anunciación. This hidden architectural gem boasts intricate details and a serene ambiance. Marvel at the delicate craftsmanship and immerse yourself in the quiet grace of this lesser-explored sanctuary.

6. El Sardinero's Secluded Coves

While El Sardinero is renowned for its main beaches, seek out the secluded coves that dot the coastline. These hidden pockets of paradise offer a more intimate beach experience, away from the crowds. Bask in the sun, dip your toes in the refreshing waters, and relish the tranquillity of these secret seaside escapes.

7. Escaleras de la Catedral's Staircase to History

Ascend the Escaleras de la Catedral, a hidden staircase that leads to breathtaking views of Santander's skyline. As you climb, each step unveils a panoramic canvas, capturing the essence of the city. This hidden vantage point is a photographer's dream and a poetic space to reflect on Santander's beauty.

8. Rincón de Menéndez Pelayo's Literary Haven

Discover Rincón de Menéndez Pelayo, a charming square that pays homage to Santander's literary legacy. This hidden gem is adorned with statues and plaques commemorating the city's literary figures. Feel the echoes of the past as you explore this haven of inspiration tucked away in the heart of Santander.

9. La Ría de Santander's Sunset Glow

Follow the meandering path along La Ría de Santander, especially during the golden hours of sunset. As the sun dips below the horizon, witness the waters of the bay reflecting the warm hues of the sky. This hidden vantage point offers a mesmerising view, where the city's silhouette becomes a silhouette painted with the palette of twilight.

10. Museo de Prehistoria y Arqueología's Time Capsule

Delve into the Museo de Prehistoria y Arqueología, a hidden gem that transports you through Santander's ancient history. This museum houses artefacts and exhibits, allowing you to step back in time and connect with the city's prehistoric roots.

Uncover the stories engraved in the remnants of Santander's past.

11. Mirador de Cabo Mayor's Coastal Panorama

Escape to the Mirador de Cabo Mayor, a hidden viewpoint offering a panoramic spectacle of Santander's coastal beauty. From here, the sweeping vistas of the sea and cliffs create a canvas that captures the essence of the city's maritime spirit. It's a quiet retreat where nature's grandeur unfolds in every direction.

12. Barrio Pesquero's Authentic Flavours

Venture into Barrio Pesquero, the Fisherman's Quarter, where authenticity thrives. Explore narrow lanes lined with seafood restaurants, where the day's catch is transformed into delectable dishes. This hidden culinary enclave allows you to savour Santander's maritime heritage through the flavours of the sea.

13. Faro de Cabo Mayor's Coastal Sentinels

Visit the Faro de Cabo Mayor, a lighthouse perched on the edge of the cliffs. Beyond its practical purpose, this hidden landmark offers breathtaking views of the rugged coastline. Hear the whispers of the sea, feel the breeze on your face, and appreciate the solitude that envelops this coastal sentinel.

14. Plaza Porticada's Architectural Elegance

Wander into Plaza Porticada, a hidden square adorned with architectural elegance. Encircled by colonnades and adorned facades, this plaza exudes a timeless charm. Unwind on a bench, soak in the ambiance, and appreciate the harmonious blend of history and modernity in this unassuming urban oasis.

As you unearth these hidden gems, let each discovery be a chapter in your personal Santander narrative. These lesser-known treasures contribute to the city's allure, promising a journey that transcends the ordinary. In Santander's hidden corners, the true essence of the city awaits, ready to captivate the intrepid traveller with its whispered tales and unexplored wonders.

Off-the-Beaten-Path

Off-the-Beaten-Path Treasures: Santander's Hidden Neighbourhoods

In the heart of Santander, where the rhythmic tides of the sea meet the echoes of history, lie neighbourhoods that often escape the spotlight but harbour the city's most authentic stories. Step away from the well-trodden paths and immerse yourself in the charm of these off-the-beaten-path quarters, where the essence of Santander awaits the curious traveller.

1. Puertochico: Nautical Whispers Amidst Tranquillity

Puertochico, a quiet harbouring neighbourhood, is a sanctuary where nautical whispers paint the air. Stroll along the marina, where small fishing boats and yachts create a picturesque scene. Amidst the tranquillity, discover hidden seafood taverns and quaint shops that beckon with maritime tales.

2. Tetuán: Bohemian Vibes and Artistic Echoes

Tetuán, with its bohemian vibes, is a canvas painted with artistic echoes. Explore narrow streets adorned with colourful murals and street art that tell the stories of Santander's creative spirit. Uncover independent galleries, quirky boutiques, and cosy cafes that add a splash of creativity to this hidden gem.

3. Canadio: Culinary Exploration Beyond the Mainstream

Canadio, a lesser-known culinary haven, invites you to embark on a gastronomic adventure. This off-the-beaten-path neighbourhood is a tapestry of traditional eateries and trendy food spots. Indulge in pintxos, sip local wines, and relish the diverse flavours that define Santander's rich culinary landscape.

4. Castilla-Hermida: A Melting Pot of Tradition and Modernity

Castilla-Hermida, a neighbourhood where tradition meets modernity, is a vibrant mosaic of local life. Navigate through bustling markets, where locals engage in daily routines, and uncover hidden squares that come alive with the city's heartbeat. Embrace the dynamic energy that emanates from this authentic Santander quarter.

5. Cueto: Coastal Charms and Seaside Serenity

Cueto, perched along the coast, is a hidden enclave where time seems to slow down. Meander through charming streets lined with colourful houses, and savour panoramic views of the Bay of Biscay. Cueto's coastal charms offer a serene escape, inviting you to immerse yourself in seaside serenity.

6. Miranda: Historic Elegance and Timeless Grace

Miranda, with its historic elegance, unveils a chapter of Santander's past. Wander through its streets, where well-preserved architecture tells tales of a bygone era. Explore the squares adorned with statues and fountains, capturing the timeless grace that defines this hidden neighbourhood.

7. San Martín: Artisanal Discoveries in Every Corner

San Martín, an artisanal treasure trove, invites you to uncover unique finds in its hidden corners. Delve into workshops and boutiques, where local artisans showcase their craftsmanship. From handmade jewellery to traditional crafts, San Martín is a neighbourhood that celebrates Santander's artistic soul.

8. Monte: Nature's Retreat Amidst Urban Splendour

Monte, a nature retreat within the city, is a hidden gem where urban splendour harmonises with green landscapes. Ascend the rolling hills to discover parks and gardens offering panoramic views of Santander. Monte is a tranquil escape, providing a peaceful respite from the bustling city below.

9. Loredo: Surfer's Paradise and Coastal Delight

Loredo, a coastal gem, beckons surf enthusiasts and those seeking seaside tranquillity alike. Venture beyond the city centre to discover sandy shores where waves dance to a rhythmic melody. Whether you're catching waves or simply basking in the coastal ambiance, Loredo is a hidden paradise along Santander's shores.

10. El Alisal: Parkland Bliss and Historic Resonance

El Alisal, nestled in the embrace of greenery, offers a haven for those seeking parkland bliss. Explore the expansive parks and gardens that define this neighbourhood, each step resonating with historic echoes. El Alisal invites you to wander through time, where nature and history intertwine in harmonious splendour.

11. Albericia: Sports Enthusiasts' Haven

Albericia, a neighbourhood pulsating with sports fervour, is a haven for enthusiasts and spectators alike. Home to sports facilities and stadiums, this off-the-beaten-path quarter captures the dynamic spirit of Santander's athletic community. Whether you're catching a match or simply soaking in the vibrant energy, Albericia is where sports enthusiasts find their playground.

12. La Pereda: Tranquil Residences and Charming Streets

La Pereda, a tranquil residential enclave, invites you to wander through charming streets adorned with elegant residences. Embrace the peaceful atmosphere as you explore this hidden neighbourhood, where the daily rhythm of life unfolds in a timeless fashion. La Pereda is a quiet retreat, offering a glimpse into Santander's residential elegance.

13. Campogiro: Rural Charms in the Heart of the City

Campogiro, a pocket of rural charm in the heart of Santander, surprises with its quaint landscapes. Meander through narrow lanes, where gardens and greenery create a picturesque ambiance. This hidden neighbourhood provides a delightful contrast to the urban surroundings, inviting you to experience a touch of the countryside within the city.

14. El Sardinero Alto: Panoramic Views and Coastal Grandeur

El Sardinero Alto, perched on elevated terrain, offers panoramic views and coastal grandeur. Ascend to hidden viewpoints that unveil breathtaking vistas of the sea and city below. This off-the-beaten-path neighbourhood allows you to marvel at Santander's beauty from a different perspective, where the landscape becomes a masterpiece to behold.

In these lesser-known corners of Santander, the city's diverse facets come to life. Each off-the-beaten-path neighbourhood is a chapter in Santander's narrative, contributing to the mosaic of experiences that define this coastal gem. As you explore these hidden quarters, may the authentic spirit of Santander captivate your senses, leaving you with a profound connection to a city that unfolds its magic beyond the expected routes.

Charming Cafés and Boutique Shops

Charming Cafés and Boutique Shops: Santander's Elegance Unveiled

Santander, with its elegant allure, invites you to savour the city's heartbeat in the embrace of charming cafés and boutique shops. Beyond the bustling streets, these hidden gems beckon with a promise of refined experiences, where each sip of coffee and every discovery in a boutique tell a tale of Santander's sophistication and cultural richness.

1. Café de las Arte: Artistry in Every Sip

Enter Café de las Arte, where each cup of coffee is a masterpiece. Nestled in the heart of Santander, this café blends the essence of a traditional coffeehouse with a gallery-like ambiance. Sip your espresso surrounded by local artwork, and let the flavours intertwine with the creative spirit that defines Santander's cultural canvas.

2. La Taza de Oro: A Coffee Legacy

La Taza de Oro, a timeless café with a storied legacy, invites you to step into an atmosphere steeped in history. The aroma of freshly brewed coffee fills the air as you immerse yourself in the charm of this café. It's not just a place to enjoy a cup; it's an invitation to be part of Santander's coffee culture, where tradition and taste converge.

3. Café Royalty: Elegance Redefined

Café Royalty, an epitome of elegance, is where Santander's past and present seamlessly blend. With its opulent décor and refined ambiance, this café is a sanctuary for those seeking a taste of sophistication. Let the baristas guide you through a coffee experience that mirrors the grandeur of this hidden gem.

4. Boutique del Pan: Culinary Artistry in Bites

Boutique del Pan, a culinary haven, goes beyond the conventional bakery. Step into a world where bread becomes a canvas for artistic expression. From artisanal pastries to freshly baked loaves, each creation reflects Santander's dedication to culinary craftsmanship. Indulge your senses in a symphony of flavours curated with precision.

5. La Máquina: Pintxos Perfected

La Máquina, a boutique eatery specialising in pintxos, is a testament to Santander's culinary artistry. This cosy establishment celebrates the flavours of the region, presenting a tapestry of small bites that are both visually enticing and gastronomically delightful. Explore the culinary landscape of Santander through these bite-sized masterpieces.

6. Librería Gil: A Literary Retreat

Librería Gil, more than just a bookstore, is a sanctuary for book lovers and connoisseurs of intellectual elegance. Sip your coffee amidst shelves lined with literary treasures, immersing yourself in the quiet sophistication of this boutique establishment. It's a place where coffee and literature intertwines, creating an atmosphere of refined relaxation.

7. Ría del Carmen: Seaside Elegance

Ría del Carmen, perched along the waterfront, is a charming café where sea breezes complement the aroma of freshly brewed coffee. With panoramic views of the bay, this hidden gem allows you to savour your espresso against a backdrop of coastal grandeur. It's a celebration of Santander's maritime spirit in every sip.

8. Niza Café: Bohemian Vibes and Coffee Aesthetics

Niza Café, exuding bohemian vibes, is a coffee haven where aesthetics meet taste. From the eclectic décor to the carefully crafted brews, this café is a testament to Santander's commitment to the art of coffee. Lose yourself in the ambiance, and let each visit be a sensory journey through the city's cultural nuances.

9. Delicatessen La Rosa: Culinary Artisanal Symphony

Delicatessen La Rosa, a culinary sanctuary, invites you to embark on an artisanal symphony of flavours. This boutique shop curates a collection of gourmet delights, from local cheeses to exquisite chocolates. Explore the shelves adorned with gastronomic treasures, and let the passionate staff guide you through a culinary journey that captures Santander's palate.

10. El Baúl del Sibarita: Curated Elegance

El Baúl del Sibarita, a hidden treasure trove, is where curated elegance takes centre stage. This boutique shop curates a selection of fine wines, gourmet delicacies, and artisanal products. Immerse yourself in the ambiance, where every item tells a story of Santander's dedication to sophistication and the finer things in life.

11. Mía Boutique: Fashion Flourish in Every Stitch

Mía Boutique, a fashion haven, is where style meets artistry. Step into this boutique shop, where carefully selected garments and accessories reflect Santander's fashion-forward spirit. Whether you're seeking a unique ensemble or a statement piece, Mía Boutique invites you to explore the city's chic side.

12. La Ría Artesanía: Handcrafted Treasures

La Ría Artesanía, a haven for lovers of handcrafted treasures, is a boutique shop where artistry takes various forms. From locally made jewellery to ceramics and textiles, each item is a testament to Santander's artisanal heritage. Let the ambiance inspire your appreciation for craftsmanship and the stories woven into each creation.

13. Casa Gispert: Aromas of Tradition

Casa Gispert, more than a shop, is a sensory journey into tradition. Known for its aromatic coffees and handcrafted nuts, this boutique establishment invites you to explore the tastes that define Santander's culinary heritage. The rich scents and flavours within Casa Gispert offer a glimpse into the city's dedication to culinary excellence.

14. Galería de Arte: Artistic Splendour Beyond Museums

Galería de Arte, a boutique art gallery, is a hidden gem where artistic splendour transcends museum walls. Discover local and international artists showcased in a space that exudes creativity. The curated exhibits in this boutique art gallery provide an intimate encounter with Santander's vibrant artistic community.

15. Paseo de Pereda's Riverside Boutiques: Elegance Along the Riverbank

Stroll along Paseo de Pereda, where boutique shops adorn the riverside with elegance. From designer boutiques to quaint stores, this picturesque promenade unveils a curated selection of fashion, jewellery, and artisanal finds. Each boutique along Paseo de Pereda contributes to the city's allure with a touch of riverside sophistication.

In these charming cafés and boutique shops, Santander's cultural heartbeat resonates. Each sip of coffee and every discovery in a boutique is an invitation to partake in the city's refined elegance. Whether you're savouring the craftsmanship in a cup or indulging in the artistic curation of a boutique, Santander's charm is unveiled in every nuanced detail, promising a journey of sophistication and cultural discovery.

Scenic Walking Trails

Santander's Scenic Walking Trails: A Symphony of Nature and Culture

Embark on a journey through Santander's scenic walking trails, where each step unveils a harmonious blend of nature's beauty and the city's rich cultural tapestry. Beyond the urban bustle, these trails invite you to explore hidden corners, panoramic vistas, and historical gems that narrate Santander's story in the language of landscapes.

1. El Sardinero Promenade: Coastal Elegance Unveiled

Begin your adventure on the El Sardinero Promenade, where the rhythmic waves of the Bay of Biscay serenade your stroll. This scenic trail along the coast offers panoramic views, gentle sea breezes, and the charming play of sunlight on the water. Feel the coastal elegance as you traverse this iconic waterfront pathway.

2. Parque de Las Llamas: Tranquil Oasis Amidst Urban Splendour

Parque de Las Llamas beckons with its lush greenery and tranquil ambiance, creating a serene oasis within the city. As you meander through the walking trails, encounter sculptures, ponds, and shaded paths that offer a peaceful retreat. This park is a testament to Santander's commitment to harmonising nature with urban splendour.

3. Jardines de Pereda: Botanical Poetry Along the Riverbank

Explore the Jardines de Pereda, where botanical poetry unfolds along the River Pisuerga. Stroll amidst vibrant flowerbeds, sculpted gardens, and shaded walkways that provide a picturesque setting. This scenic trail invites you to immerse yourself in the beauty of nature while enjoying the cultural nuances reflected in the riverside landscape.

4. Peninsula de la Magdalena: Historical Charms and Coastal Tranquillity

The Peninsula de la Magdalena offers a walking trail where historical charms meet coastal tranquillity. Amidst lush gardens and regal buildings, follow the path that unveils breathtaking views of the Cantabrian Sea. This scenic journey through history and nature is a captivating experience that captures the essence of Santander.

5. Cabo Mayor Coastal Path: Cliffs, Lighthouses, and Maritime Majesty

Embark on the Cabo Mayor Coastal Path, where cliffs meet lighthouses, and maritime majesty unfolds. This trail along the rugged coastline provides awe-inspiring vistas of the Bay of

Biscay. Hear the soothing sounds of crashing waves as you traverse this scenic route, offering a close encounter with Santander's maritime grandeur.

6. Faro de Cabo Mayor to Playa de Matalenas: Seaside Splendour

Walk from Faro de Cabo Mayor to Playa de Matalenas, tracing a route along the cliffs and secluded coves. This scenic journey showcases the diverse landscapes of Santander's coastline. Revel in the panoramic views, breathe in the salty sea air, and let the seaside splendour enchant your senses.

7. Sendero de la Braguía: Forested Bliss and Mountainous Views

For a nature-infused adventure, explore the Sendero de la Braguía, where forested bliss meets mountainous views. Wander through shaded trails, hear the rustling of leaves, and witness the changing scenery as you ascend. This scenic walking trail offers a refreshing escape into the natural wonders surrounding Santander.

8. Paseo de Canalejas: Urban Elegance with a Historical Flair

Paseo de Canalejas invites you to experience urban elegance with a historical flair. As you stroll along this picturesque avenue, framed by stately buildings and charming squares, immerse yourself in the architectural beauty that narrates Santander's history. This scenic walking trail offers a cultural journey within the city's heart.

9. Parque Natural de Peña Cabarga: Hiking Amidst Verdant Beauty

For those seeking a more challenging adventure, explore the Parque Natural de Peña Cabarga. This natural park boasts hiking trails amidst verdant landscapes and panoramic viewpoints. As you ascend, the sweeping vistas unfold, providing a rewarding experience that harmonises Santander's natural beauty with outdoor exploration.

10. Costa Quebrada Coastal Path: Dramatic Cliffs and Turquoise Waters

Venture along the Costa Quebrada Coastal Path, where dramatic cliffs meet turquoise waters. This scenic trail showcases the rugged beauty of Santander's coastline, offering unparalleled views of the Cantabrian Sea. Wander along the cliffside paths and feel the awe-inspiring grandeur of this coastal masterpiece.

11. Parque Natural de las Dunas de Liencres: Coastal Dunes and Untouched Beauty

Discover the Parque Natural de las Dunas de Liencres, where coastal dunes and untouched beauty create a haven for nature enthusiasts. Follow the winding trails through golden sands, explore the unique ecosystems, and witness the meeting point of land and sea. This scenic walking trail is a journey into the pristine landscapes that define Santander's coastal allure.

12. Ruta de los Faros: Lighthouse Trail along the Cliffs

Immerse yourself in the Ruta de los Faros, a lighthouse trail that winds along the cliffs, offering unparalleled coastal panoramas. As you navigate this scenic path, encounter historic lighthouses that stand as silent sentinels overlooking the vast expanse of the Bay of Biscay. The Ruta de los Faros is a visual symphony of Santander's maritime heritage.

13. Paseo de la Reina Victoria: Historic Elegance Along the Bay

Stroll along the Paseo de la Reina Victoria, a scenic trail that exudes historic elegance along the bay. Lined with majestic buildings and lush greenery, this waterfront promenade provides a tranquil escape. Admire the architecture, breathe in the sea breeze, and let the ambiance narrate tales of Santander's regal past.

14. Senda Fluvial del Pas: Riverside Retreat with Countryside Views

The Senda Fluvial del Pas invites you to a riverside retreat with countryside views. This scenic walking trail follows the meandering Pas River, offering glimpses of rural landscapes and charming villages. Wander through shaded paths, cross quaint bridges, and experience the serenity that characterises this tranquil riverside route.

15. Camino Lebaniego: Pilgrim's Path to Spiritual Tranquillity

For those seeking a spiritual and scenic journey, explore the Camino Lebaniego. This historic pilgrimage trail connects Santander to the Monastery of Santo Toribio de Liébana. Walk amidst lush landscapes, picturesque villages, and rolling hills, experiencing the spiritual tranquillity that has drawn pilgrims for centuries.

16. Monte Buciero Coastal Walk: Cliff-top Views and Maritime Majesty

The Monte Buciero Coastal Walk invites you to traverse cliff-top paths with expansive views of the Bay of Santander. This scenic trail offers a perfect blend of nature and maritime majesty, where each step unveils a panoramic spectacle of the coastal wonders. Revel in the beauty of Santander's bay from this elevated vantage point.

17. Senda Fluvial de Besaya: Riverside Serenity Near Santander

Enjoy riverside serenity along the Senda Fluvial de Besaya, a scenic walking trail near Santander. Follow the meandering Besaya River, surrounded by lush greenery and charming landscapes. This trail provides a peaceful escape, allowing you to reconnect with nature just a short distance from the city.

18. Paseo de Menéndez Pelayo: Maritime Stroll with Cultural Flair

Paseo de Menéndez Pelayo offers a maritime stroll with a cultural flair. As you walk along this scenic avenue, adorned with historic buildings and seaside charm, soak in the cultural ambiance. This trail captures the essence of Santander's coastal elegance, making it a delightful journey through both nature and history.

19. Senda Fluvial de Miera: Riverside Retreat Amidst Green Valleys

Experience a riverside retreat amidst green valleys along the Senda Fluvial de Miera. This scenic trail follows the Miera River, meandering through verdant landscapes and picturesque countryside. Revel in the tranquillity, listen to the babbling river, and let the natural beauty of Santander's hinterland unfold around you.

20. Camino de Santiago del Norte: Coastal Pilgrimage with Ocean Views

Join the Camino de Santiago del Norte, a coastal pilgrimage route that offers ocean views and cultural richness. This scenic walking trail follows the northern coast, allowing you to absorb the beauty of Santander's shoreline while embracing the pilgrimage traditions that have shaped this historic path.

Santander's scenic walking trails weave a tapestry of landscapes, from coastal promenades to historic avenues, inviting you to explore the city's natural and cultural treasures on foot.

CHAPTER FOUR

Santander's Top Attractions

Santander's Top Attractions: A Kaleidoscope of Cultural and Natural Wonders

Dive into the captivating charm of Santander as you explore its top attractions, where each landmark tells a story of cultural richness and natural beauty. From historic sites that echo tales of the past to scenic wonders that showcase the city's coastal allure, Santander's top attractions promise a kaleidoscope of experiences that will linger in your memories.

Historic Landmarks

Santander's Historic Landmarks: Echoes of Time amidst Modern Elegance

Step into the heart of Santander's rich history as you explore its historic landmarks, where architectural marvels and cultural treasures stand as testaments to the city's enduring legacy. From regal palaces that witnessed centuries of aristocratic splendour to cathedrals that embody Gothic grandeur, Santander's historic landmarks weave a narrative that seamlessly blends the past with the city's modern elegance.

1. Palacio de la Magdalena: Coastal Regality Amidst Gardens

Palacio de la Magdalena, a coastal gem, reigns atop the Peninsula de la Magdalena. This regal palace, with its eclectic architecture, has witnessed epochs of royalty. Wander through its majestic halls, traverse manicured gardens, and relive the elegance of Santander's aristocratic past against the backdrop of breathtaking sea views.

2. Catedral de Santander: Gothic Splendour in Stone

The Catedral de Santander, a Gothic masterpiece, graces the city's skyline with its intricate stone façade and towering spires. Step inside to marvel at its serene interior, adorned with religious art and centuries-old craftsmanship. The cathedral stands as a spiritual beacon, echoing with centuries of devotion and architectural splendour.

3. Iglesia de Santa Lucía: Hidden Gem of Cueto

Iglesia de Santa Lucía, a hidden gem in the neighbourhood of Cueto, showcases a blend of Gothic and Renaissance architecture. This church, with its ornate facade and historical significance, invites you to step back in time and appreciate the religious and artistic heritage that characterises Santander's lesser-known treasures.

4. Palacio de Riva-Herrera: Neo-Gothic Elegance in the City Centre

Palacio de Riva-Herrera, an emblem of Neo-Gothic elegance, graces the city centre with its intricate details and soaring spires. This historic palace, surrounded by urban charm, tells a tale of aristocratic refinement and architectural grandeur. Explore its façade and immerse yourself in the atmosphere of Santander's bygone era.

5. Antiguo Hospital de San Rafael: Baroque Grandeur Preserved

The Antiguo Hospital de San Rafael stands as a testament to Baroque grandeur, its façade preserving the essence of the city's architectural history. This historic building, once a hospital, now adds a touch of timeless elegance to Santander's streets. Wander through its surroundings and let the echoes of the past captivate your senses.

6. Palacete del Embarcadero: Belle Époque Splendour by the Sea

Palacete del Embarcadero, an architectural jewel of the Belle Époque era, stands by the sea, exuding splendour and sophistication. This palatial structure, with its ornate details and seaside setting, captures the essence of a bygone era. Immerse yourself in its elegance and appreciate the fusion of history and coastal allure.

7. Palacio de Festivales de Cantabria: Modern Cultural Icon

The Palacio de Festivales de Cantabria, though modern, has become a cultural icon in Santander. This architectural marvel hosts artistic performances and events, contributing to the city's contemporary cultural landscape. Its sleek design and cultural significance make it a landmark that bridges the historical and the modern in Santander.

8. Plaza Porticada: Neoclassical Splendour in the Heart

Plaza Porticada, a neoclassical square in the heart of Santander, is surrounded by stately buildings that showcase architectural splendour. As you stroll through the plaza, admire the Porticada structures and appreciate the historic significance of this urban hub. Plaza Porticada is a living canvas that paints a picture of Santander's neoclassical elegance.

9. Palacio de Exposiciones y Congresos de Santander: Modern Architectural Marvel

The Palacio de Exposiciones y Congresos de Santander, a modern architectural marvel, stands as a testament to the city's contemporary design. With its sleek lines and innovative structure, this venue hosts cultural and business events, embodying Santander's commitment to modernity while respecting its historic context.

10. Banco de Santander Building: Financial Legacy in Stone

The Banco de Santander Building, a symbol of the city's financial legacy, stands as a testament to Santander's economic history. This iconic structure, with its robust stone exterior and intricate detailing, reflects the solidity and endurance that define the financial institution it represents. As you gaze upon its facade, you witness the intersection of finance and architectural grandeur.

11. Monumento a José María de Pereda: Literary Tribute in Bronze

The Monumento a José María de Pereda, a bronze tribute, honours the literary legacy of one of Santander's notable authors. This monument, adorned with intricate details, stands as a reminder of the city's cultural contributions. As you observe the sculpture, you connect with the literary spirit that permeates Santander's history.

12. Muralla de Santander: Remnants of Ancient Fortifications

The Muralla de Santander, remnants of ancient fortifications, whisper tales of Santander's mediaeval past. These weathered stone walls, scattered throughout the city, evoke images of a bygone era when defences were built to safeguard against external threats. As you encounter sections of the mediaeval walls, you glimpse into Santander's historical resilience.

13. Estación Marítima: Maritime Gateway with Architectural Flair

The Estación Marítima, a maritime gateway, combines functionality with architectural flair. This modern structure, serving as a port terminal, seamlessly integrates into Santander's waterfront. Its design reflects the city's commitment to blending utility with aesthetics, creating a symbolic entry point that welcomes travellers arriving by sea.

14. Monumento a Los Raqueros: Homage to Seafaring Traditions

The Monumento a Los Raqueros pays homage to Santander's seafaring traditions and the resilience of its people. This sculpture, depicting children diving into the sea for coins, stands as a poignant reminder of the city's maritime heritage. As you observe this artistic tribute, you connect with the spirit of Santander's coastal communities.

15. Palacio de Justicia: Legal Elegance in Urban Surroundings

Palacio de Justicia, a courthouse exuding legal elegance, graces Santander's urban surroundings. The architectural finesse of this building reflects the importance of justice within the city. As you pass by, the Palacio de Justicia stands as a symbol of legal authority, seamlessly blending into the fabric of Santander's civic architecture.

16. Casa-Museo Menéndez Pelayo: Literary Sanctuary

Casa-Museo Menéndez Pelayo, once the residence of the renowned author Marcelino Menéndez Pelayo, is a literary sanctuary preserving the legacy of this influential figure. This historic house, with its period furnishings and literary artefacts, invites you to step into the world of Menéndez Pelayo and appreciate the cultural contributions of Santander's literary luminaries.

17. Edificio de Correos y Telégrafos: Architectural Postcard of History

Edificio de Correos y Telégrafos, the post office building, is an architectural postcard that encapsulates a slice of Santander's history. The grandeur of its design reflects the significance of communication in the city's past. As you gaze upon this historical structure, you envision an era when letters and telegrams played pivotal roles in connecting Santander to the world.

18. Monumento a Juan de la Cosa: Nautical Homage

The Monumento a Juan de la Cosa, a nautical homage, celebrates the life of the famous cartographer and explorer. This monument, situated by the sea, captures the spirit of adventure and discovery that defines Santander's maritime legacy. As you stand before the statue, you feel a connection to the city's seafaring past.

19. Antiguo Ayuntamiento: Civic Heritage in the Heart of Santander

The Antiguo Ayuntamiento, the old town hall, is a civic heritage nestled in the heart of Santander. This historic building, with its charming architecture, has witnessed moments of civic significance. As you admire its facade, you sense the civic pride that emanates from this structure, symbolising the governance and history of Santander.

Santander's historic landmarks, each with its unique story and architectural allure, create a mosaic of the city's cultural identity. As you explore these treasures, you'll find echoes of time harmoniously blending with modern elegance, inviting you to witness the evolving narrative of Santander's rich and storied past.

Natural Wonders

Santander's Natural Wonders: A Symphony of Coastal Beauty and Lush Landscapes

Embark on a journey through Santander's natural wonders, where the city's beauty is seamlessly intertwined with the breathtaking landscapes that surround it. From the mesmerising coastline that embraces the Bay of Biscay to the verdant parks and trails that cradle the city, Santander's natural wonders are a testament to the harmonious coexistence of urban sophistication and pristine nature.

1. Bay of Biscay: Coastal Majesty Unveiled

The Bay of Biscay, a masterpiece of coastal majesty, unfolds along Santander's shores. Gaze upon the vast expanse of turquoise waters meeting the rugged cliffs, and feel the rhythmic dance of waves. The bay is not merely a body of water; it is a living canvas that captures the essence of Santander's maritime allure.

2. El Sardinero Beaches: Sun, Sand, and Seaside Serenity

El Sardinero beaches, a duo of sandy stretches, invite you to indulge in the sun, sand, and seaside serenity. Whether you're basking in the warmth of the sun, taking a leisurely stroll along the promenade, or embracing the refreshing sea breeze, El

Sardinero epitomises the laid-back charm that defines Santander's coastal lifestyle.

3. Parque Natural de las Dunas de Liencres: Coastal Dunas and Untouched Beauty

The Parque Natural de las Dunas de Liencres beckon nature enthusiasts with its coastal dunes and untouched beauty. Wander through golden sands, explore unique ecosystems, and witness the meeting point of land and sea. This natural haven is a sanctuary where the pristine landscapes define Santander's coastal allure.

4. Peninsula de la Magdalena: Historical Charms and Coastal Tranquillity

The Peninsula de la Magdalena offers historical charms amidst coastal tranquillity. Explore lush gardens, regal buildings, and breathtaking views of the Cantabrian Sea.

This peninsula is not just a geographic feature; it's a testament to Santander's commitment to preserving natural beauty alongside its historical legacy.

5. Cabo Mayor Coastal Path: Cliffs, Lighthouses, and Maritime Majesty

Embark on the Cabo Mayor Coastal Path, where cliffs meet lighthouses, and maritime majesty unfolds. This trail along the rugged coastline provides awe-inspiring vistas of the Bay of Biscay.

Hear the soothing sounds of crashing waves as you traverse this scenic route, offering a close encounter with Santander's maritime grandeur.

6. Parque de la Vaguada de las Llamas: Nature's Haven in the City

Parque de la Vaguada de las Llamas is a nature haven nestled within the city, offering a retreat into green landscapes and serene ponds. This expansive park is a sanctuary for relaxation, outdoor activities, and picnics. Escape the urban hustle and immerse yourself in the tranquillity of Santander's green oasis.

7. Jardines de Piquío: Botanical Beauty by the Sea

Jardines de Piquío, a botanical gem by the sea, invites you to stroll through lush gardens that frame stunning coastal views. This idyllic retreat offers a perfect blend of natural beauty and artistic landscapes. Relax in the shade of centuries-old trees, breathe in the sea breeze, and savour the tranquillity of this enchanting haven.

8. Parque Natural de Peña Cabarga: Hiking Amidst Verdant Beauty

For those seeking a more challenging adventure, explore the Parque Natural de Peña Cabarga. This natural park boasts hiking trails amidst verdant landscapes and panoramic viewpoints. As you ascend, the sweeping vistas unfold, providing a rewarding experience that harmonises Santander's natural beauty with outdoor exploration.

9. Parque de Matalenãs: Coastal Park with Breathtaking Views

Parque de Matalenãs, a coastal park, beckons with its natural beauty and breathtaking views of the Bay of Santander. Traverse the walking trails, enjoy the sea breeze, and marvel at the coastal panoramas that unfold from this vantage point. The park is a serene retreat where nature and urban charm converge.

10. Costa Quebrada Coastal Path: Dramatic Cliffs and Turquoise Waters

Venture along the Costa Quebrada Coastal Path, where dramatic cliffs meet turquoise waters. This scenic trail showcases the rugged beauty of Santander's coastline, offering unparalleled views of the Cantabrian Sea. Wander along the cliff-side paths and feel the awe-inspiring grandeur of this coastal masterpiece.

11. Ría de Cubas: Estuarine Beauty and Biodiversity

The Ría de Cubas, an estuarine marvel, showcases the beauty of brackish waters and diverse ecosystems. This tidal inlet not only adds a picturesque element to Santander's landscapes but also provides a habitat for a rich variety of flora and fauna. Explore its shores, witness the changing tides, and appreciate the natural harmony that characterises this estuarine wonder.

12. Senda Fluvial del Pas: Riverside Retreat with Countryside Views

The Senda Fluvial del Pas invites you to a riverside retreat with countryside views. This scenic walking trail follows the meandering Pas River, offering glimpses of rural landscapes and charming villages. Wander through shaded paths, cross quaint bridges, and experience the serenity that characterises this tranquil riverside route.

13. Monte Buciero: Cliff-top Panoramas and Maritime Majesty

Monte Buciero, rising majestically along the coast, offers cliff-top panoramas and maritime majesty. This natural wonder provides an elevated vantage point to absorb the beauty of the Bay of Santander. Explore its trails, revel in the coastal breeze, and let the rugged cliffs narrate tales of geological wonder that have unfolded over millennia.

14. Senda Fluvial de Besaya: Riverside Serenity Near Santander

Enjoy riverside serenity along the Senda Fluvial de Besaya, a scenic walking trail near Santander. Follow the meandering Besaya River, surrounded by lush greenery and charming landscapes. This trail provides a peaceful escape, allowing you to reconnect with nature just a short distance from the city.

15. Parque Natural de Oyambre: Coastal and Countryside Harmony

The Parque Natural de Oyambre harmonises coastal beauty with countryside landscapes. This natural park, a short distance from Santander, unveils pristine beaches, rolling hills, and vibrant flora. Immerse yourself in the diverse ecosystems, from sand dunes to forests, creating a tapestry of natural wonders that characterise the region.

16. Parque Natural de las Marismas de Santoña, Victoria y Joyel: Wetland Wonderland

The Parque Natural de las Marismas de Santoña, Victoria y Joyel is a wetland wonderland that unfolds along the Bay of Biscay. This protected area is a haven for birdwatchers and nature enthusiasts. Traverse its wooden walkways, observe migratory birds, and witness the intricate beauty of marshes that play a vital role in the region's biodiversity.

17. Senda Fluvial de Miera: Riverside Retreat Amidst Green Valleys

Experience a riverside retreat amidst green valleys along the Senda Fluvial de Miera. This scenic trail follows the Miera River, meandering through verdant landscapes and picturesque countryside. Revel in the tranquillity, listen to the babbling river, and let the natural beauty of Santander's hinterland unfold around you.

18. Parque Natural de las Collados del Asón: Karstic Wonders and Waterfalls

The Parque Natural de las Collados del Asón captivates with karstic wonders and cascading waterfalls. This natural park is a playground of geological marvels, from limestone formations to deep gorges. Hike through its trails, marvel at the subterranean landscapes, and feel the energy of water carving its way through millennia.

19. Parque Natural de las Secuoyas del Monte Cabezón: Majestic Giants Amidst Forest Tranquillity

The Parque Natural de las Secuoyas del Monte Cabezón is home to majestic giants amidst forest tranquillity. Walk among towering sequoias, witness the awe-inspiring height of these ancient trees, and feel the serenity that emanates from this unique natural sanctuary. It's a peaceful retreat where the grandeur of nature takes centre stage.

20. Playa de Covachos: Secluded Beach Bliss

Playa de Covachos, a secluded beach, offers blissful solitude amidst pristine nature. Nestled between cliffs, this hidden gem welcomes you with golden sands and turquoise waters. Accessible by a scenic hike, it rewards intrepid explorers with a secluded coastal haven, where the sounds of waves and the beauty of nature create a serene escape.

Santander's natural wonders paint a diverse canvas, from coastal splendours to inland retreats, inviting you to immerse yourself in the beauty that defines this enchanting city and its surrounding landscapes. Each natural wonder is a chapter in the love story between Santander and nature, inviting you to explore and cherish the unique harmony that unfolds in every corner of this coastal gem.

Adventure Palette

Santander's Adventure Palette: Thrills and Exploration Await

Embark on an exhilarating journey through Santander's adventure activities, where the city's dynamic landscapes provide the backdrop for adrenaline-pumping experiences and outdoor exploration. From the sparkling waters of the Bay of Biscay to the lush hinterlands, Santander invites thrill-seekers to dive into a myriad of activities that promise not only excitement but also a deeper connection with the natural wonders that surround this vibrant city.

1. **Surfing on El Sardinero Beach: Ride the Cantabrian Waves**

El Sardinero Beach becomes a playground for surf enthusiasts, inviting you to ride the Cantabrian waves. Whether you're a seasoned surfer or a beginner catching your first break, the energy of the ocean and the lively atmosphere of El Sardinero create the perfect setting for an exhilarating surf adventure.

2. **Kayaking in the Bay of Biscay: Paddle along Santander's Coastline**

Kayaking in the Bay of Biscay offers a unique perspective of Santander's coastline. Glide over the gentle waves, explore hidden coves, and marvel at the cityscape from the water. This adventure activity provides not only a physical workout but also a tranquil escape surrounded by the beauty of the sea.

3. Mountain Biking in Parque Natural de Peña Cabarga: Trails for Thrill-Seekers

Parque Natural de Peña Cabarga becomes a haven for mountain biking enthusiasts, offering trails that wind through lush landscapes and challenge your biking skills. Feel the rush as you navigate rugged terrain, enjoy panoramic views, and experience the thrill of downhill descents in this natural adventure playground.

4. Hiking the Costa Quebrada Coastal Path: Cliff-top Trails and Ocean Vistas

Hiking the Costa Quebrada Coastal Path presents adventure seekers with cliff-top trails and ocean vistas. This scenic route combines the excitement of trekking with breathtaking views of the Cantabrian Sea. Each step is a journey into Santander's coastal grandeur, where the trail unfolds like a story waiting to be explored.

5. Scuba Diving in the Bay of Santander: Underwater Exploration

Scuba diving in the Bay of Santander unveils a world of underwater wonders. Dive beneath the surface to discover marine life, explore hidden rock formations, and witness the vibrant colours of the underwater ecosystem. This adventure activity provides a unique perspective of Santander's coastal biodiversity.

6. Rock Climbing in Monte Buciero: Ascend Cliffs with Coastal Panoramas

Monte Buciero offers a rock-climbing paradise where enthusiasts can ascend cliffs with panoramic coastal views. Feel the exhilaration as you conquer rock faces, experience the thrill of reaching new heights, and savour the breathtaking vistas of Santander's bay unfolding beneath you.

7. Windsurfing in Playa de los Bikinis: Harness the Cantabrian Wind

Playa de los Bikinis becomes a windsurfing haven, where thrill-seekers harness the power of the Cantabrian wind. Glide over the waves, master the art of balancing on the board, and feel the adrenaline rush as you navigate the open waters. It's a dynamic adventure that combines skill and the sheer joy of riding the wind.

8. Caving in the Karstic Caves of Parque Natural de las Collados del Asón: Subterranean Exploration

The Karstic Caves of Parque Natural de las Collados del Asón invite adventurers to delve into subterranean exploration. Navigate through intricate caverns, marvel at stalactite formations, and experience the mysterious beauty that lies beneath the surface. Caving in this natural park is a journey into the Earth's hidden wonders.

9. Paragliding Over the Costa Quebrada: Soar Above Coastal Beauty

Paragliding over the Costa Quebrada allows you to soar above Santander's coastal beauty. Experience the rush of adrenaline as you glide through the air, marvel at the cliffs and beaches below, and appreciate the unique perspective that paragliding offers of Santander's picturesque landscapes.

10. Horseback Riding in Parque Natural de Oyambre: Equestrian Adventures

Parque Natural de Oyambre becomes a backdrop for equestrian adventures, inviting horseback riding enthusiasts to explore its diverse landscapes. Canter along sandy beaches, traverse rolling hills, and immerse yourself in the tranquillity of nature while experiencing the timeless joy of horseback riding.

11. Sailing on the Cantabrian Sea: Nautical Excursions and Seafaring Thrills

Sailing on the Cantabrian Sea transforms your visit into a nautical adventure. Feel the wind in your sails as you navigate the open waters, absorbing the coastal beauty from the deck of your sailboat. Whether you're a seasoned sailor or a novice, Santander's maritime allure provides the perfect setting for an unforgettable sailing experience.

12. Stand-Up Paddle-boarding in the Ría de Cubas: Serene Exploration on the Water

Stand-Up Paddle-boarding in the Ría de Cubas offers a serene and immersive way to explore Santander's waterways. Glide along the estuary, paddle at your own pace, and soak in the tranquillity of the surroundings. This activity combines balance and relaxation, allowing you to connect with the natural beauty of the Ría de Cubas.

13. Zip Lining in Parque Natural de Peña Cabarga: Treetop Thrills and Aerial Views

Zip lining in Parque Natural de Peña Cabarga adds a thrilling dimension to your adventure. Soar through the tree-tops, experience the rush of the wind, and enjoy aerial views of the natural park. This exhilarating activity combines adrenaline with the scenic beauty of Santander's landscapes.

14. Canyoning in the Gorges of Parque Natural de las Collados del Asón: Adrenaline Amidst Waterfalls

Canyoning in the gorges of Parque Natural de las Collados del Asón is an adrenaline-fuelled adventure amidst waterfalls and rock formations. Descend through narrow canyons, navigate cascading water, and experience the thrill of exploration in this unique natural setting. Canyoning in Santander is a journey into the heart of untamed landscapes.

15. Off-Road Jeep Safari in the Hinterlands: Explore Santander's Interior

An off-road Jeep safari in Santander's hinterlands takes you on an exploration of the city's interior. Venture off the beaten path, traverse rugged terrains, and witness the diversity of landscapes that define Santander beyond its coastal allure. This adventure allows you to discover hidden gems and connect with the city's hinterland.

16. Kitesurfing on Playa de Matalenas: Harness the Wind and Waves

Kitesurfing on Playa de Matalenas invites thrill-seekers to harness the synergy of wind and waves. Feel the adrenaline surge as you ride the waves propelled by a kite, mastering the art of balance and control. The open waters of Matalenas provide an ideal playground for kitesurfing enthusiasts seeking aquatic excitement.

17. Bungee Jumping from Puente Colgante: Adrenaline from a Historic Bridge

Bungee jumping from Puente Colgante, a historic suspension bridge, adds an exhilarating twist to your Santander adventure. Take a leap from the bridge, experience the heart-pounding freefall, and enjoy a unique perspective of the city as you dangle above the water. This adrenaline-packed activity is a daring way to create lasting memories in Santander.

18. Fishing Excursion in the Bay of Santander: Maritime Relaxation with a Twist

A fishing excursion in the Bay of Santander offers a unique blend of maritime relaxation and excitement. Cast your line into the tranquil waters, enjoy the sea breeze, and revel in the anticipation of a catch. This activity provides a leisurely yet rewarding experience, connecting you with the city's maritime traditions.

19. Hot Air Ballooning Over Santander: Aerial Serenity and Panoramic Views

Hot air ballooning over Santander transforms your adventure into an aerial serenity. Drift above the city and its surroundings, enjoying panoramic views of the coastline, parks, and historic landmarks. The gentle ascent provides a serene contrast to the thrilling vistas, creating a unique and memorable experience.

20. Archery in Parque de la Vaguada de las Llamas: Precisión Amidst Nature

Archery in Parque de la Vaguada de las Llamas combines precision with the tranquillity of nature. Hone your archery skills amidst green landscapes, breathe in the fresh air, and enjoy the meditative quality of this ancient sport. Archery in Santander is an activity that blends focus, relaxation, and the natural beauty of the city's parks.

Santander's adventure offerings are as diverse as its landscapes, promising excitement, and exploration at every turn. Whether you seek the thrill of the sea, the challenge of the mountains, or the serenity of the skies, Santander invites you to embrace the spirit of adventure and create lasting memories in this dynamic and captivating city.

CHAPTER FIVE

Stellar Accommodations

Santander's Stellar Accommodations: Where Comfort Meets Coastal Elegance

Discover the epitome of comfort and luxury in Santander's stellar accommodations, where each establishment is a sanctuary that harmonises with the city's coastal charm. From boutique hotels with panoramic sea views to historic gems nestled in the heart of the city, Santander's accommodations promise not only a restful stay but an immersive experience that reflects the city's unique blend of sophistication and maritime allure.

Luxury Hotels

Santander's Opulent Retreats: Luxury Hotels Redefined

Indulge in the lap of luxury amidst Santander's opulent retreats, where every detail is meticulously crafted to elevate your stay into an unforgettable experience. From sumptuous suites with panoramic views to world-class amenities and personalised service, these luxury hotels redefine hospitality, offering a haven of sophistication within the enchanting embrace of Santander's coastal allure.

1. Hotel Real: The Crown Jewel of Seaside Elegance

Hotel Real stands as the crown jewel of seaside elegance, a timeless sanctuary overlooking the Bay of Santander. With opulent rooms, Michelin-starred dining, and a spa that exudes tranquillity, this luxury haven seamlessly blends historic grandeur with contemporary indulgence, promising an unparalleled experience of refinement by the sea.

2. Eurostars Hotel Real: Modern Splendour in Historic Surroundings

Eurostars Hotel Real marries modern splendour with historic surroundings, offering a luxurious escape near El Sardinero Beach. Immerse yourself in its lavish rooms, savour gourmet cuisine, and unwind in the spa. This luxury retreat combines sophistication with the allure of Santander's coastal landscape.

3. Gran **Hotel Sardinero: Coastal Grandeur and Refined Comfort**

Gran Hotel Sardinero epitomises coastal grandeur and refined comfort, inviting guests to luxuriate in its sumptuous ambiance. From the regal decor to the panoramic views of the Cantabrian

Sea, this luxury hotel sets the stage for an extraordinary experience where every moment is steeped in elegance.

4. Vincci Puertochico: Boutique Chic and Unparalleled Service

Vincci Puertochico embodies boutique chic and unparalleled service, creating an intimate luxury haven by the marina. With individually designed rooms, rooftop terraces, and a commitment to personalised excellence, this hotel redefines boutique luxury in the heart of Santander.

5. Hotel Bahía Santander: Contemporary Elegance on the Waterfront

Hotel Bahía Santander offers contemporary elegance on the waterfront, a haven where luxury meets the rhythms of the Bay of Biscay. Indulge in modern comfort, relish gourmet dining, and experience the seamless blend of sophistication and coastal allure that defines this luxurious retreat.

6. Silken Coliseum: Urban Sophistication and Central Grandeur

Silken Coliseum exudes urban sophistication and central grandeur, a luxurious retreat in the heart of Santander. With sleek design, cutting-edge amenities, and proximity to cultural treasures, this hotel offers an oasis of refinement where the city's vibrant energy meets opulent tranquillity.

7. Hotel Real Palacio de la Magdalena: Royal Splendour by the Sea

Hotel Real Palacio de la Magdalena unveils royal splendour by the sea, a luxury retreat nestled near the historic Peninsula de la Magdalena. Immerse yourself in the lavish interiors, enjoy exclusive access to the royal stables, and experience the regal charm that defines this opulent haven.

8. Eurostars Hotel Real Palacio de la Magdalena: Secluded Luxury Amidst Nature

Eurostars Hotel Real Palacio de la Magdalena offers secluded luxury amidst nature, an exclusive retreat surrounded by the Peninsula de la Magdalena's natural beauty. With spacious suites, private terraces, and direct access to pristine beaches, this hotel creates an intimate haven for those seeking a tranquil escape.

9. Hospes Palacio del Marqués de Santillana: Historical Opulence in the Old Town

Hospes Palacio del Marqués de Santillana invites guests to historical opulence in the old town, a boutique hotel housed in a meticulously restored palace. With lavish suites, a spa that echoes Santander's coastal tranquillity and a commitment to personalised service, this hotel is a sanctuary of luxury in Santander's historic core.

10. Eurostars Hotel Santander Parayas: Modern Luxury with Airport Convenience

Eurostars Hotel Santander Parayas offers modern luxury with airport convenience, providing a seamless blend of comfort and accessibility. With spacious rooms, contemporary design, and proximity to Santander Airport, this hotel ensures a luxurious respite for travellers seeking both style and convenience.

11. Hotel Boutique Las Brisas: Intimate Seaside Elegance

Hotel Boutique Las Brisas extends an invitation to intimate seaside elegance, where personalised service and meticulous attention to detail redefine luxury. Nestled away from the bustle, this boutique gem creates an oasis of tranquillity, offering individually designed rooms and a serene garden retreat. Immerse yourself in the artistry of hospitality at Las Brisas for an exclusive coastal experience.

12. Hotel Art Santander: Avant-Garde Luxury and Creative Expression

Hotel Art Santander stands as a testament to avant-garde luxury and creative expression, where each corner is adorned with contemporary artworks. This hotel is a gallery of modern design, offering guests a unique fusion of comfort and culture. Immerse yourself in the vibrant spirit of Santander from the stylish surroundings of Hotel Art Santander.

13. Posada Casa de Valle: Rustic Luxury with Mountain Views

Posada Casa de Valle presents rustic luxury with mountain views, a charming retreat that blends elegance with the tranquillity of the Cantabrian Mountains. This posada offers a unique escape into nature, providing comfortable rooms, a garden oasis, and a serene atmosphere for those seeking a luxurious connection to the countryside.

14. Posada Las Garzas: Secluded Coastal Charm

Posada Las Garzas is a haven of secluded coastal charm, offering a peaceful escape by the sea. Nestled in natural surroundings, this posada invites guests to relax in a tranquil setting, with personalised service and a connection to the pristine beauty of Santander's coastline. Experience the luxury of seclusion at Posada Las Garzas.

15. Hotel City House Alisas: Cultural Proximity with Modern Comfort

Hotel City House Alisas combines cultural proximity with modern comfort, creating a luxurious retreat near Santander's artistic hubs. This hotel, with its sleek design and comfortable accommodations, offers a refined escape for guests seeking both style and a connection to the city's vibrant arts scene.

16. Gran Hotel Victoria: Coastal Grandeur with Panoramic Vistas

Gran Hotel Victoria epitomises coastal grandeur with panoramic vistas; a luxury retreat perched on the edge of the Bay of Santander. Indulge in opulent rooms, gourmet dining, and expansive sea views that create a mesmerising backdrop for a truly luxurious experience by the water.

17. Hotel Chiqui: Coastal Boutique Experience

Hotel Chiqui presents a coastal boutique experience, where the intimate ambiance meets the grandeur of seaside landscapes. With personalised service, stylish interiors, and proximity to El

Sardinero Beach, this hotel is a chic haven for those seeking luxury infused with the rhythmic charm of the Bay of Biscay.

18. Hotel Piñamar: Sea-view Comfort in the Residential Area

Hotel Piñamar offers sea-view comfort in Santander's residential area, a family-run establishment that combines cosy ambiance with panoramic views. With comfortable rooms and a location near the beach, this hotel creates a luxurious retreat for guests seeking a serene coastal escape.

19. Hotel Marqués de Santillana: Historical Splendour in the Old Town

Hotel Marqués de Santillana invites guests to historical splendour in Santander's old town, a luxury escape housed in a meticulously restored building. With a commitment to preserving architectural charm while offering modern amenities, this hotel provides a unique blend of comfort and historical richness.

20. Hotel Santander Parayas: Airport Convenience with Modern Comfort

Hotel Santander Parayas provides airport convenience without compromising on modern comfort, a luxury retreat designed for seamless travel. With contemporary design, spacious rooms, and proximity to Santander Airport, this hotel ensures a luxurious respite for travellers seeking both style and convenience.

Santander's luxury hotels are not merely places to stay; they are immersive experiences that celebrate the city's unique blend of sophistication and coastal allure. Each establishment, whether perched by the sea or nestled in historic quarters, promises a haven of indulgence, inviting guests to savour the extraordinary at every turn.

Bed and Breakfast Charm

Santander's Cosy Retreats: Bed and Breakfast Charm

Nestled within the heart of Santander, these charming bed and breakfasts offer more than just a place to stay; they provide a warm embrace of hospitality and a unique connection to the city's soul. From quaint rooms adorned with local charm to the personal touch of attentive hosts, these cosy retreats invite you to experience Santander in an intimate and authentic way.

1. Hospedaje Magallanes: Quaint Elegance in the Historic Quarter

Hospedaje Magallanes exudes quaint elegance in Santander's historic quarter. This charming bed and breakfast, with its historic architecture and cosy interiors, offers a unique blend of comfort and tradition. Immerse yourself in the charm of

Santander's old town from the welcoming embrace of Hospedaje Magallanes.

2. Posada Casa de Valle: Rural Tranquillity with Mountain Views

Posada Casa de Valle provides rural tranquillity with views of the Cantabrian Mountains. This charming posada offers a retreat into nature, with comfortable rooms, a garden oasis, and proximity to hiking trails. Experience the serenity of rural Santander at Posada Casa de Valle.

3. Hotel Piñamar: Sea-view Comfort in the Residential Area

Hotel Piñamar offers sea-view comfort in Santander's residential area. This family-run bed and breakfast combines a cosy ambiance with panoramic views. With comfortable rooms and a location near the beach, Hotel Piñamar creates a charming retreat for those seeking a serene coastal escape.

4. Posada Las Garzas: Secluded Coastal Charm

Posada Las Garzas offers secluded coastal charm, providing a peaceful escape by the sea. Nestled in natural surroundings, this posada invites you to relax in a tranquil setting, with personalised service and a connection to the pristine beauty of Santander's coastline. Experience the luxury of seclusion at Posada Las Garzas.

5. Hotel City House Alisas: Cultural Proximity with Modern Comfort

Hotel City House Alisas combines cultural proximity with modern comfort, creating a cosy retreat near Santander's artistic hubs. With its sleek design and comfortable accommodations, this bed and breakfast offers a refined escape for guests seeking both style and a connection to the city's vibrant arts scene.

6. Gran Hotel Victoria: Coastal Grandeur with Panoramic Vistas

Gran Hotel Victoria epitomises coastal grandeur with panoramic vistas; a charming bed and breakfast perched on the edge of the Bay of Santander. Indulge in opulent rooms, gourmet dining, and expansive sea views that create a mesmerising backdrop for a truly cosy experience by the water.

7. Hotel Chiqui: Coastal Boutique Experience

Hotel Chiqui presents a coastal boutique experience, where the intimate ambiance meets the grandeur of seaside landscapes. With personalised service, stylish interiors, and proximity to El Sardinero Beach, this bed and breakfast is a chic haven for those seeking cosy luxury infused with the rhythmic charm of the Bay of Biscay.

8. Posada el Angel de la Guarda: Quaint Charm in the Countryside

Posada el Angel de la Guarda exudes quaint charm in the Santander countryside. This posada, with its rustic elegance and peaceful surroundings, offers a unique escape from the urban hustle. Immerse yourself in the beauty of the countryside while enjoying the warm hospitality of Posada el Angel de la Guarda.

9. Hotel Boutique Las Brisas: Intimate Seaside Retreat

Hotel Boutique Las Brisas invites you to an intimate seaside retreat, where personalised service meets coastal serenity. Tucked away from the bustle, this boutique gem offers individually designed rooms, a tranquil garden, and a proximity to the beaches of Somo. Immerse yourself in the charm of Las Brisas for a secluded coastal escape.

10. Posada Casa de Valle: Rural Tranquillity with Mountain Views

Posada Casa de Valle provides rural tranquillity with views of the Cantabrian Mountains. This charming posada offers a retreat into nature, with comfortable rooms, a garden oasis, and proximity to hiking trails. Experience the serenity of rural Santander at Posada Casa de Valle.

Santander's bed and breakfasts, with their unique personalities and genuine warmth, ensure that your stay is not just a pause in your journey but an integral part of your Santander experience. Whether you choose a historic quarter, a seaside view, or a hidden garden, these cosy retreats promise a delightful blend of comfort and local charm.

Budget-Friendly Gems

Santander's Budget-Friendly Gems: Affordable Comfort and Local Flavour

Explore Santander without breaking the bank by choosing from these budget-friendly options that prioritise affordability without compromising on comfort or local charm. From hostels with a vibrant atmosphere to budget hotels with strategic locations, these gems offer a wallet-friendly way to experience the beauty and culture of Santander.

1. Hostal Liebana: Wallet-Friendly Warmth in the Heart of Santander

Hostal Liebana combines wallet-friendly warmth with a central location, providing a welcoming haven in the heart of Santander. With cosy rooms and a commitment to affordable comfort, this hostel invites budget-conscious travellers to enjoy the genuine hospitality that defines the city's character.

2. Hostal Jardin Secreto: Affordable Tranquillity in Santander's City Centre

Hostal Jardin Secreto unfolds as an affordable haven of tranquillity in Santander's city centre, offering a charming escape that won't strain your budget. Nestled in a historic building, this budget-friendly option features cosy rooms and a hidden garden, providing a peaceful retreat amidst the city's vibrant energy.

3. Hospedaje Santander: Historic Charm on a Budget

Hospedaje Santander radiates historic charm on a budget, a delightful accommodation option nestled in the heart of the old town. With cosy rooms and affordable rates, this Hospedaje allows budget-conscious travellers to immerse themselves in

Santander's cultural treasures without compromising on comfort.

4. Hostal Vintage Santander: Retro Elegance at an Affordable Price

Hostal Vintage Santander boasts retro elegance at an affordable price, inviting guests to experience a unique and budget-friendly atmosphere. With vintage decor and reasonable rates, this hostel offers a cosy and affordable stay in Santander's maritime quarter.

5. Hostal Rocamar: Budget-Friendly Sea-View Serenity in El Sardinero

Hostal Rocamar provides budget-friendly sea-view serenity in El Sardinero, offering a cosy retreat by the beach without breaking the bank. With affordable rates and rooms that capture panoramic views of the Bay of Biscay, this budget option allows guests to enjoy coastal tranquillity on a budget.

6. Hostal La Torre: Budget-Friendly Quaint Elegance in the Historic Quarter

Hostal La Torre radiates budget-friendly quaint elegance in Santander's historic quarter, blending affordability with a touch of historic allure. With comfortable rooms and wallet-friendly rates, this hostel offers an accessible option for budget-conscious travellers seeking the charm of the old town.

7. Hostal La Marina: Maritime Charm by the Port on a Budget

Hostal La Marina captures maritime charm by the port on a budget, providing a cosy and budget-friendly stay that reflects Santander's seafaring spirit. With nautical-inspired decor and affordable rates, this budget option offers a delightful retreat for travellers without compromising on comfort.

8. Hostal La Victoria: Hidden Gem in the City Centre on a Budget

Hostal La Victoria stands as a hidden gem in Santander's city centre on a budget, offering affordable comfort away from the bustling streets. With personalised service and wallet-friendly rates, this hostel creates an intimate retreat for budget-conscious travellers exploring the city's attractions.

9. Hostal San Fernando: Affordable Comfort with a Homely Touch

Hostal San Fernando provides affordable comfort with a homely touch, presenting budget-conscious travellers with a welcoming and budget-friendly option. With simple yet cosy rooms and wallet-friendly rates, this hostel offers a cost-effective and inviting place to stay in Santander.

10. Pensión Angelines: Budget-Friendly Accommodation with Local Flavour

Pensión Angelines stands as a budget-friendly accommodation option with local flavour, providing affordable comfort in a welcoming atmosphere. With a central location and reasonable rates, this pension invites budget-conscious travellers to experience the authentic spirit of Santander without breaking the bank.

11. Hostal Castilla Santander: Affordable Lodging with City Convenience

Hostal Castilla Santander offers affordable lodging with city convenience, presenting budget-conscious travellers with a comfortable stay in a central location. With straightforward accommodations and reasonable rates, this hostel ensures accessibility and ease for guests exploring Santander's urban delights.

12. Hostal Del Carmen: Budget-Friendly Haven in El Sardinero

Hostal Del Carmen serves as a budget-friendly haven in El Sardinero, providing affordable accommodations by the seaside. With a welcoming atmosphere and reasonable rates, this hostel allows budget-conscious travellers to enjoy the coastal charm of Santander without compromising on affordability.

13. Hostal San Glorio: Cosy Retreat in a Budget-Friendly Setting

Hostal San Glorio offers a cosy retreat in a budget-friendly setting, creating a warm and affordable haven for travellers exploring Santander. With comfortable rooms and wallet-friendly rates, this hostel ensures that guests can experience the city's allure without straining their budget.

14. Hostal Cabo Mayor: Affordable Stay with Views of Santander's Iconic Lighthouse

Hostal Cabo Mayor provides an affordable stay with views of Santander's iconic lighthouse, offering budget-conscious travellers a comfortable option with a touch of coastal charm. With straightforward accommodations and wallet-friendly rates, this hostel allows guests to soak in the scenic beauty of Santander without breaking the bank.

15. Hostal Del Pozo: Budget-Friendly Lodging in the Heart of Santander

Hostal Del Pozo stands as a budget-friendly lodging option in the heart of Santander, presenting guests with affordable comfort in a central location. With simplicity and reasonable rates, this hostel ensures that budget-conscious travellers can explore the city's cultural treasures with ease.

16. Hostal Plaza: Affordable Accommodations near Santander's Main Square

Hostal Plaza offers affordable accommodations near Santander's main square, providing budget-conscious travellers with a convenient and comfortable stay. With a central location and wallet-friendly rates, this hostel allows guests to immerse themselves in the city's vibrant atmosphere without exceeding their budget.

17. Hostal de Cabo Menor: Coastal Comfort on a Budget

Hostal de Cabo Menor provides coastal comfort on a budget, offering affordable accommodations with a seaside touch. With straightforward rooms and budget-friendly rates, this hostel invites guests to experience Santander's coastal allure without compromising on affordability.

18. Hostal Stella Maris: Budget-Friendly Seaside Retreat

Hostal Stella Maris serves as a budget-friendly seaside retreat, presenting guests with affordable accommodations in proximity to the beach. With a welcoming atmosphere and reasonable rates, this hostel ensures that budget-conscious travellers can enjoy the coastal ambiance of Santander without breaking the bank.

19. Hostal Balmoral: Affordable Lodging with a Homely Atmosphere

Hostal Balmoral provides affordable lodging with a homely atmosphere, creating a welcoming space for budget-conscious travellers. With comfortable rooms and wallet-friendly rates, this hostel ensures that guests can enjoy a cosy and budget-friendly stay in the heart of Santander.

20. Hostal del Nilo: Budget-Friendly Accommodations in El Sardinero

Hostal del Nilo offers budget-friendly accommodations in El Sardinero, providing an affordable option for travellers seeking comfort by the sea. With a friendly ambiance and reasonable rates, this hostel allows guests to explore Santander's coastal charm without straining their budget.

Santander's budget-friendly options cater to savvy travellers, offering affordable comfort and a taste of local life. Whether you choose a central location, seaside views, or a cosy retreat, these accommodations ensure that your stay in Santander is not only memorable but also cost-effective.

CHAPTER SIX

Museums and Experiences

Santander's Cultural Tapestry: Museums and Experiences

Immerse yourself in Santander's rich cultural tapestry, where history, art, and heritage converge to create a captivating journey. Explore the city's museums and cultural experiences that unveil the soul of Santander, inviting you to witness its fascinating stories and artistic expressions.

Art Galleries

Santander's Artistic Odyssey: Galleries of Expression

Embark on an artistic odyssey in Santander, where creativity takes centre stage in the city's vibrant art galleries. From contemporary masterpieces to avant-garde exhibitions, explore the diverse expressions of Santander's artistic soul in these captivating galleries.

1. Galería Siboney: Contemporary Art Haven in the Old Town

Galería Siboney stands as a contemporary art haven in the old town, showcasing the works of both established and emerging artists. With its eclectic exhibitions and a commitment to pushing artistic boundaries, this gallery invites you to immerse yourself in the dynamic and ever-evolving world of contemporary art.

2. Espacio Alexandra: Fusion of Art and Innovation

Espacio Alexandra is a fusion of art and innovation, providing a platform for artists who blur the lines between traditional and modern expressions. This gallery's commitment to pushing artistic boundaries creates an immersive experience that captivates the imagination and challenges conventional perceptions of art.

3. Galería Juan Silió: A Tapestry of Modern and Avant-Garde Art

Galería Juan Silió weaves a tapestry of modern and avant-garde art, featuring a diverse collection that reflects the ever-changing landscape of artistic expression. With exhibitions that transcend traditional boundaries, this gallery invites you to explore the cutting edge of contemporary art in the heart of Santander.

4. La Nave Que Late: Artistic Exploration in a Cultural Hub

La Nave Que Late is a cultural hub for artistic exploration, where creativity knows no bounds. This dynamic space hosts exhibitions, installations, and performances, creating an immersive environment that encourages dialogue between artists and the community, fostering a vibrant and evolving cultural scene.

5. Galería Cànem Santander: A Tapestry of Modern and Avant-Garde Art

Galería Cànem Santander, an extension of the renowned gallery in Castellón, brings a tapestry of modern and avant-garde art to the Cantabrian coast. With a commitment to showcasing diverse artistic expressions, this gallery provides a window into the contemporary art scene both locally and internationally.

6. Centro de Arte Faro Cabo Mayor: Coastal Inspiration for Artistic Expression

Centro de Arte Faro Cabo Mayor draws coastal inspiration for artistic expression, situated in a lighthouse overlooking the Bay of Santander. This unique gallery space showcases the intersection of art and the sea, inviting visitors to experience the transformative power of creative expression against the backdrop of coastal beauty.

7. Galería Vanguardia: Bridging Tradition and Innovation

Galería Vanguardia serves as a bridge between tradition and innovation, featuring a diverse collection that celebrates the rich heritage of Spanish art while embracing contemporary visions. With its carefully curated exhibitions, this gallery creates a space where the past and present coalesce in a harmonious celebration of artistic expression.

8. La Fábrica: Industrial Chic Meets Artistic Exploration

La Fábrica melds industrial chic with artistic exploration, transforming a former factory into a dynamic space for contemporary art. This gallery's commitment to showcasing experimental works and pushing the boundaries of artistic expression adds a layer of innovation to Santander's cultural landscape.

9. Galería Espacio Luz: Illuminating Artistic Expression

Galería Espacio Luz is dedicated to illuminating artistic expression, providing a platform for artists whose works transcend conventional boundaries.

With a focus on showcasing innovative and thought-provoking art, this gallery invites visitors to experience the transformative power of light and creativity.

10. Arte Santander: Annual Showcase of Contemporary Art

Arte Santander serves as an annual showcase of contemporary art, bringing together galleries, artists, and art enthusiasts in a celebration of creativity. This art fair contributes to Santander's cultural vibrancy, providing a dynamic platform for the exploration and appreciation of cutting-edge artistic expressions.

11. Sala Robayera: Rural Charm Meets Artistic Expression

Sala Robayera embodies a unique fusion where rural charm meets artistic expression. Nestled in a picturesque setting, this gallery provides a serene backdrop for exhibitions that celebrate the connection between art and nature, inviting visitors to experience the transformative power of creativity in a tranquil environment.

12. Galería Concha Pedrosa: Showcasing Regional Artistic Talent

Galería Concha Pedrosa takes pride in showcasing regional artistic talent, providing a platform for local artists to shine. With a focus on nurturing and promoting the creative voices of Santander, this gallery contributes to the city's cultural identity by fostering a strong connection between artists and their community.

13. Estación Marítima Santander: Contemporary Art by the Waterfront

Estación Marítima Santander brings contemporary art to the waterfront, utilising a unique space to showcase artistic expressions against the backdrop of the sea. This gallery invites visitors to experience the convergence of art and maritime beauty, creating a dynamic dialogue between creativity and the natural environment.

14. Sala Bretón: A Cultural Gem in the Heart of Santander

Sala Bretón stands as a cultural gem in the heart of Santander, providing a space for artistic exhibitions that reflect the city's vibrant spirit. With a rotating display of works from local and international artists, this gallery contributes to the cultural mosaic of Santander, creating a dynamic hub for creative exploration.

15. Factoría del Arte: Creative Hub for Emerging Talents

Factoría del Arte emerges as a creative hub for emerging talents, offering a platform for young and innovative artists to showcase their works. With a focus on nurturing creativity and providing exposure to rising stars in the art world, this gallery contributes to Santander's cultural landscape by fostering the next generation of artistic voices.

16. La **Garúa: Artistic Storm in a Contemporary Space**

La Garúa represents an artistic storm in a contemporary space, where experimental and challenging works find a home. This gallery embraces the unpredictable and tempestuous nature of artistic expression, inviting visitors to experience the exhilaration of creativity that transcends traditional boundaries.

17. Espacio Creativo Alexandra: Artistic Fusion in a Collaborative Setting

Espacio Creativo Alexandra embodies artistic fusion in a collaborative setting, where artists come together to explore innovative and interdisciplinary works. This dynamic space fosters a sense of community and encourages dialogue between creators, adding a layer of collaborative energy to Santander's artistic scene.

18. Galería Maverick: Pushing the Boundaries of Visual Arts

Galería Maverick is dedicated to pushing the boundaries of visual arts, showcasing works that challenge conventional perspectives. With a focus on contemporary and experimental creations, this gallery invites visitors to engage with art that transcends traditional norms, sparking curiosity and redefining the limits of visual expression.

19. Casa Rábago: Historic Venue for Contemporary Art

Casa Rábago transforms a historic venue into a space for contemporary art, blending the charm of the past with the innovation of the present. This gallery celebrates the intersection of history and modernity, offering visitors a unique journey through time as they explore the diverse and dynamic works on display.

Santander's art galleries form a kaleidoscopic panorama of creativity, where traditional, contemporary, and avant-garde expressions converge to shape the city's cultural landscape. Each gallery, with its distinct personality and commitment to artistic exploration, contributes to Santander's identity as a thriving hub of creative inspiration.

Historical Museums

Santander's Tapestry of Time: Historical Museums Unveiled

Delve into the rich tapestry of Santander's history by exploring its captivating historical museums. From ancient artefacts to immersive exhibits, these museums offer a journey through time, allowing you to unravel the stories and heritage that have shaped the city into the vibrant cultural hub it is today.

1. Museo de Prehistoria y Arqueología de Cantabria: Gateway to Ancient Cantabria

Museo de Prehistoria y Arqueología de Cantabria serves as the gateway to ancient Cantabria, inviting you to explore archaeological wonders that span from the Palaeolithic era to the Roman period. The museum's comprehensive collection, including replicas of the famous Altamira cave, offers a fascinating glimpse into the prehistoric roots of the region.

2. Museo Marítimo del Cantábrico: Nautical Chronicles and Maritime Heritage

Museo Marítimo del Cantábrico unfolds nautical chronicles and maritime heritage, immersing visitors in the seafaring history of Santander. From ship models to artefacts, this museum provides a captivating journey through the city's connection to the Cantabrian Sea, offering insights into the lives of sailors and the evolution of maritime trade.

3. Museo Regional de Prehistoria y Arqueología de Cantabria: Reliving the Past

Museo Regional de Prehistoria y Arqueología de Cantabria invites you to relive the past, showcasing archaeological treasures that narrate the cultural evolution of Cantabria. This museum provides a comprehensive overview of the region's history, from early human settlements to the influences of Roman civilization, offering a vivid narrative of Cantabria's historical journey.

4. Museo de la Ciudad: Chronicle of Urban Evolution

Museo de la Ciudad unfolds the chronicle of urban evolution, offering a glimpse into the development of Santander through the ages. Housed in the former Banco de España building, this museum presents historical artefacts, photographs, and exhibits that trace the architectural and cultural metamorphosis of the city.

5. Palacio de la Magdalena: Royal Resonance and Coastal Elegance

Palacio de la Magdalena resonates with royal history and coastal elegance, inviting visitors to explore the majestic palace overlooking the Bay of Santander. The guided tours provide a regal experience, unravelling the history and grandeur of the palace, which has witnessed the presence of royalty and played a vital role in Santander's past.

6. Ermita de la Virgen del Mar: Spiritual Sanctuary with Coastal Views

Ermita de la Virgen del Mar stands as a spiritual sanctuary with coastal views, offering a unique blend of religious history and natural beauty. This hermitage invites you to experience the tranquil ambiance, admire the Cantabrian coast, and discover the spiritual significance embedded in the charming surroundings.

7. Iglesia Catedral de Nuestra Señora de la Asunción: Gothic Grandeur in the Heart of Santander

Iglesia Catedral de Nuestra Señora de la Asunción, the cathedral, showcases Gothic grandeur in the heart of Santander. Marvel at its architectural splendour, explore its chapels, and absorb the spiritual richness that echoes through centuries within the walls of this iconic religious landmark.

8. Museo Municipal de Bellas Artes de Santander: Artistic Legacy in a Noble Residence

Museo Municipal de Bellas Artes de Santander celebrates the artistic legacy housed in a noble residence, once the home of the Marquis of Valdecilla. This museum, adorned with elegant rooms, features a diverse collection of Cantabrian artists, offering a unique perspective on the regional artistic heritage within an aristocratic setting.

9. Biblioteca y Casa-Museo Menéndez Pelayo: Literary Haven of a Spanish Scholar

Biblioteca y Casa-Museo Menéndez Pelayo stands as a literary haven dedicated to the Spanish scholar and writer Marcelino Menéndez Pelayo. Explore the extensive library collection, discover the writer's personal artefacts, and immerse yourself in the intellectual atmosphere of this cultural gem nestled in the heart of Santander.

10. Monumento a José María de Pereda: Tribute to a Cantabrian Novelist

Monumento a José María de Pereda pays tribute to the Cantabrian novelist, featuring sculptures that celebrate his literary contributions. Located in the Pereda Gardens, this monument honours the legacy of Pereda and his impact on Spanish literature, creating a cultural connection between the city and its literary heritage.

Santander's historical museums weave together a narrative that spans prehistoric times to the more recent chapters of urban development and cultural evolution. Each museum unfolds a unique aspect of Santander's history, inviting you to step into the footsteps of ancient inhabitants, maritime adventurers, and cultural luminaries who have left an indelible mark on the cityscape.

Interactive Cultural Events

Santander's Dynamic Rendezvous: Interactive Cultural Events

Immerse yourself in Santander's cultural vibrancy through a myriad of interactive events that transcend traditional boundaries. From lively festivals to immersive performances, these events invite you to engage, participate, and become an integral part of the city's dynamic cultural tapestry.

1. **Festival Internacional de Santander (FIS): A Global Celebration of the Arts**

The Festival Internacional de Santander (FIS) transforms the city into a global celebration of the arts. This annual event features world-class performances, from classical concerts to contemporary dance, offering a cultural feast that transcends borders. Join the international audience as Santander becomes a stage for artistic excellence and cultural exchange.

2. **Santander Music: Rhythmic Harmony by the Bay**

Santander Music creates rhythmic harmony by the bay, turning the city into a vibrant stage for music enthusiasts. This music festival features diverse genres, from indie to electronic beats, attracting both local talent and international artists. Join the crowd, feel the energy, and let the music resonate against the backdrop of Santander's coastal beauty.

3. Noche Blanca: A Night of Artistic Revelry

Noche Blanca, or White Night, transforms Santander into a nocturnal canvas of artistic revelry. This event brings together visual arts, performances, and cultural activities that span the entire city. As night falls, immerse yourself in the creative energy that illuminates the streets, squares, and cultural venues, turning Santander into a captivating nocturnal spectacle.

4. La Maruca Vive: Maritime Traditions and Coastal Celebrations

La Maruca Vive brings maritime traditions and coastal celebrations to life, turning the neighbourhood of La Maruca into a cultural hotspot. Experience interactive activities, live performances, and festivities that celebrate the city's connection to the sea. Join locals and visitors alike in embracing the vibrant spirit of Santander's coastal heritage.

5. Festival Internacional de Títeres de Santander: Puppetry Extravaganza

The Festival Internacional de Títeres de Santander is a puppetry extravaganza that captivates audiences of all ages. This event showcases the art of puppetry through interactive shows, workshops, and street performances. Join the enchanting world of puppets and experience the magic that unfolds during this lively and imaginative festival.

6. Santander Design Week: Creative Dialogues and Design Exhibitions

Santander Design Week sparks creative dialogues and design exhibitions, inviting participants to explore the intersection of art, innovation, and aesthetics. Engage in interactive workshops, attend design talks, and witness exhibitions that showcase the evolving design landscape in Santander. This week-long event fosters a dynamic exchange of ideas and celebrates the city's design prowess.

7. Feria del Libro de Santander: Literary Extravaganza by the Sea

Feria del Libro de Santander is a literary extravaganza by the sea, turning the city into a haven for book lovers. Explore book fairs, author signings, and literary discussions against the backdrop of Santander's coastal charm. Join the celebration of literature, engage with authors, and discover the diverse literary offerings that enrich the cultural fabric of Santander.

8. Santander Negro: Mysteries, Crime Fiction, and Cultural Intrigue

Santander Negro is a festival that delves into mysteries, crime fiction, and cultural intrigue. Engage in interactive crime-solving activities, attend literary discussions, and explore the darker side of literature. This event transforms Santander into a thrilling stage where mystery enthusiasts can immerse themselves in the intrigue of detective stories.

9. La Noche Europea de los Investigadores: European Researchers' Night

La Noche Europea de los Investigadores, or European Researchers' Night, turns Santander into a hub of scientific exploration and discovery. Engage in interactive experiments, attend talks by researchers, and participate in hands-on activities that showcase the wonders of science. Join the city in celebrating knowledge, curiosity, and the fascinating world of research.

10. Santander Creativa: Fostering Innovation and Cultural Expression

Santander Creativa is a dynamic initiative that fosters innovation and cultural expression. Engage in workshops, collaborative projects, and interactive exhibitions that showcase the city's commitment to creativity. Join the community of artists, entrepreneurs, and cultural enthusiasts who come together to explore new ideas and push the boundaries of innovation.

11. Santander Film Festival: Cinematic Exploration and Cultural Dialogue

Santander Film Festival invites cinephiles to a cinematic exploration and cultural dialogue. Immerse yourself in a diverse selection of films, ranging from international productions to local gems. Engage in discussions, attend screenings, and witness the power of storytelling through the lens of filmmakers from around the world.

12. Festival Internacional de Santander En Femenino: Celebrating Women in the Arts

Festival Internacional de Santander En Femenino celebrates women in the arts, featuring performances, exhibitions, and discussions that highlight the contributions of women across artistic disciplines. Engage in interactive sessions, explore exhibitions by female artists, and join the celebration of women's creativity in Santander.

13. Santander Fashion Week: Style, Innovation, and Runway Glamour

Santander Fashion Week unfolds as a showcase of style, innovation, and runway glamour. Experience the intersection of fashion and culture through runway shows, designer exhibitions, and interactive fashion events. Immerse yourself in the evolving trends and creative expressions that define Santander's position in the world of fashion.

14. Santander International Short Film Week: A Cinematic Extravaganza

Santander International Short Film Week is a cinematic extravaganza that brings together filmmakers and film enthusiasts. Attend screenings of short films from around the world, participate in discussions with filmmakers, and embrace the diversity of storytelling in a compact yet impactful format. Join the celebration of short films and cinematic creativity.

15. Santander Art Week: Exploring Contemporary Art in Various Forms

Santander Art Week is a multidimensional exploration of contemporary art in various forms. Engage in interactive art installations, attend gallery exhibitions, and participate in discussions that delve into the evolving landscape of visual expression. Immerse yourself in the dynamic and ever-changing world of contemporary art during this week-long celebration.

16. Festival Internacional de Jazz de Santander: Harmonic Notes and Musical Fusion

Festival Internacional de Jazz de Santander fills the air with harmonic notes and musical fusion, bringing jazz enthusiasts together for an unforgettable experience. Enjoy live performances by renowned jazz artists, participate in jam sessions, and feel the rhythmic pulse of Santander as it becomes a hub for jazz aficionados and musicians alike.

17. Santander Digital Week: Exploring the Intersection of Technology and Culture

Santander Digital Week explores the intersection of technology and culture through a series of interactive events, workshops, and exhibitions. Engage in discussions on digital innovation, attend tech-driven performances, and explore the evolving relationship between technology and artistic expression. Join the city in embracing the digital age with a cultural lens.

18. Santander Street Art Festival: Urban Canvases and Creative Expression

Santander Street Art Festival transforms urban spaces into canvases for creative expression. Witness the city's walls come alive with vibrant street art, participate in mural painting workshops, and explore the dynamic world of urban art. This festival celebrates the intersection of street culture and artistic innovation, turning Santander into an open-air gallery.

19. Santander Gastronomy Week: Culinary Exploration and Flavourful Delights

Santander Gastronomy Week is a culinary exploration that invites food enthusiasts to savour flavourful delights. Engage in interactive cooking classes, attend tastings by local chefs, and explore the diverse gastronomic scene of Santander. Immerse yourself in the city's culinary heritage during this week-long celebration of food and flavours.

Santander's calendar of interactive cultural events creates a vibrant tapestry of experiences, inviting locals and visitors alike to actively participate in the city's artistic, culinary, and creative endeavours.

CHAPTER SEVEN

Rich Culture

Santander's Cultural Tapestry: A Rich Mosaic of Tradition and Innovation

Santander's cultural identity is a rich mosaic woven from threads of tradition and innovation, creating a tapestry that reflects the city's deep-rooted heritage and dynamic spirit. From age-old customs to cutting-edge artistic expressions, Santander's cultural landscape invites exploration, celebration, and a profound connection with the heartbeat of the city.

1. Festivals that Reverberate

Santander's festivals, like echoes through time, resonate with a cultural fervour that transcends generations. Whether it's the Festival Internacional de Santander showcasing global artistic excellence or the vibrant Santander Music Festival pulsating with rhythmic beats, each event becomes a living chapter in the city's cultural narrative.

2. Architectural Grandeur

Architectural marvels adorn Santander's skyline, each structure whispering tales of bygone eras. From the Gothic grandeur of the Iglesia Catedral de Nuestra Señora de la Asunción to the coastal elegance of the Palacio de la Magdalena, the city's buildings are not just edifices but guardians of its cultural history.

3. Time-Honoured Traditions

In the cobbled streets and bustling markets, Santander's time-honoured traditions come to life. Whether it's the rhythmic melodies of folk music echoing through Plaza Porticada or the culinary delights of the Mercado del Este, these traditions are a living testament to the city's cultural continuity.

4. Literary Legacies

Santander's literary legacy unfolds like the pages of a cherished novel, with the Biblioteca y Casa-Museo Menéndez Pelayo standing as a literary haven. The Plaza de Pombo, surrounded by historical buildings, becomes a literary square where the echoes of great writers blend seamlessly with the city's historic charm.

5. Maritime Connections

The sea has sculpted Santander's identity, creating a cultural bond that is as deep as the ocean itself. Museo Marítimo del Cantábrico and La Maruca Vive celebrate the city's maritime heritage, offering insights into the lives of sailors, the ebb and flow of coastal traditions, and the resilient spirit shaped by the Cantabrian Sea.

6. Artistic Expressions Unleashed

Santander's commitment to the arts unfolds in a kaleidoscope of expressions. From the avant-garde creations showcased in Galería Siboney Arte to the collaborative energy of Espacio Creativo Alexandra, the city's galleries serve as portals where artistic innovation is nurtured, celebrated, and shared.

7. Culinary Symphony

Santander's culinary scene is a symphony of flavours, blending traditional recipes with contemporary gastronomy. Whether exploring the culinary crossroads of Mercado del Este or savouring the delights of Santander Gastronomy Week, the city's gastronomic offerings are a feast for the senses, embodying the essence of cultural fusion.

8. Interactive Cultural Dialogues

Santander's cultural dialogues are not confined to passive observation but invite active participation. Festivals like Noche Blanca transform the city into a canvas where everyone becomes an artist, and events like Santander Creativa foster interactive exchanges, creating a cultural ecosystem that thrives on collaboration.

9. Creative Fusion of Technology

In Santander, tradition harmonises with innovation, and this creative fusion is evident in events like Santander Digital Week. Here, the intersection of technology and culture becomes a playground for exploration, reflecting the city's commitment to staying at the forefront of contemporary creative expression.

10. Inclusive Family Celebrations

Santander's rich culture is a celebration for all, and events like Santander Kids ensure that cultural exploration is inclusive and accessible. Families come together to share in the wonders of art, science, and creativity, fostering a sense of wonder and curiosity in the youngest members of the community.

11. Street Art Renaissance

Santander experiences a renaissance through its vibrant street art scene, where urban spaces transform into open-air galleries. The Santander Street Art Festival becomes a canvas for creative expression, inviting artists to paint the city's walls with colourful murals that tell stories of diversity, resilience, and the city's evolving cultural identity.

12. Collaborative Innovation

Santander's commitment to collaborative innovation is exemplified in events like Santander Creativa. This initiative becomes a catalyst for the convergence of artistic minds, entrepreneurs, and cultural enthusiasts, fostering a dynamic environment where ideas flourish, boundaries are pushed, and innovation becomes an integral part of the city's cultural DNA.

13. Cultural Heritage Preservation

Santander stands as a guardian of its cultural heritage, preserving historical landmarks like the Iglesia Catedral de Nuestra Señora de la Asunción and the Palacio de la Magdalena. These architectural gems not only narrate the city's past but also serve as pillars of cultural continuity, reminding residents and visitors alike of the importance of preserving cultural legacies.

14. Coastal Inspirations

The coastal beauty of Santander becomes an enduring muse for artists, poets, and creators. Jardines de Piquío, with its sculpture gardens overlooking the sea, encapsulates the essence of coastal inspirations. Here, the marriage of art and nature creates a serene backdrop, inviting contemplation and reflection in harmony with the city's maritime heritage.

15. Technological Integration in Festivals

Santander's festivals seamlessly integrate technology, enhancing the cultural experience for participants. Events like Santander Digital Week bring together the realms of technology and culture, offering interactive exhibitions, virtual performances, and cutting-edge installations. This technological integration reflects the city's forward-thinking approach to cultural celebrations.

16. Inclusive Cultural Platforms

Santander embraces inclusivity through cultural platforms like Santander Kids, where families engage in interactive festivities. By providing inclusive spaces for cultural exploration, the city ensures that its rich heritage and creative expressions are accessible to people of all ages, fostering a sense of community and shared cultural experiences.

16. Cultural Diplomacy

Santander engages in cultural diplomacy by hosting international events like the Festival Internacional de Santander. This cultural exchange not only brings global artistic talent to the city but also positions Santander as a cultural hub on the international stage, promoting cross-cultural understanding and collaboration.

17. Preservation of Maritime Traditions

Santander's Museo Marítimo del Cantábrico become a guardian of maritime traditions, preserving the stories of seafaring communities. Through exhibits, interactive displays, and educational programs, the museum ensures that the cultural heritage tied to the Cantabrian Sea is celebrated and passed down to future generations.

18. Fusion of Culinary Traditions

Santander's culinary scene mirrors the city's cultural diversity, with the Mercado del Este serving as a melting pot of flavours. Here, culinary traditions blend seamlessly, creating a gastronomic tapestry that reflects the city's history, influences, and commitment to preserving the essence of traditional recipes.

19. Cultural Sustainability

Santander's rich culture is sustained through a delicate balance of preservation and innovation. The city's commitment to cultural sustainability ensures that traditions are honoured while providing space for creative expressions to evolve. This dynamic equilibrium becomes the heartbeat of Santander's cultural vitality.

In Santander, culture is not a static entity but a dynamic force that weaves through the city's past, present, and future. The commitment to inclusivity, innovation, and preservation creates a cultural tapestry that invites everyone to participate, celebrate, and contribute to the ongoing narrative of this captivating coastal city.

Local Cuisine and Culinary Delights

Santander's Culinary Symphony: A Melange of Coastal Flavours and Culinary Delights

Santander's gastronomic landscape is a captivating journey through coastal flavours, culinary traditions, and a symphony of tastes that reflect the city's vibrant spirit. From the bustling Mercado del Este to the quaint cafés by the sea, Santander's local cuisine is a celebration of freshness, creativity, and a deep connection to the bounties of the Cantabrian region.

1. Mercado del Este: Culinary Crossroads by the Sea

At the heart of Santander's culinary tapestry lies Mercado del Este, a bustling marketplace that stands as a culinary crossroads by the sea. Here, stalls overflow with vibrant produce, fresh seafood, and local delicacies, inviting both locals and visitors to embark on a sensory journey through the diverse flavours of Cantabria.

2. Mariscada Santanderina: Seafood Extravaganza

The Mariscada Santanderina is a seafood extravaganza that showcases the city's deep-rooted connection to the sea. Indulge in a platter adorned with the freshest catch of the day, succulent prawns, delectable crab, and tender clams. This culinary delight is a testament to Santander's commitment to preserving and elevating its maritime traditions.

3. Cocido Montañés: Hearty Mountain Stew

Cocido Montañés is a hearty mountain stew that warms the soul and pays homage to Santander's inland culinary traditions. Packed with chorizo, morcilla (blood sausage), beans, and greens, this comforting dish reflects the influence of the Cantabrian Mountains on the city's gastronomic heritage.

4. Rabas: Crispy Calamari Delight

Rabas, or crispy calamari, is a local favourite that captures the essence of Santander's coastal charm. Savour the delightfully crunchy texture as you bite into these golden rings of calamari, often accompanied by a zesty aioli. It's a seaside snack that perfectly encapsulates the freshness of Cantabrian seafood.

5. Anchoas de Santander: Treasured Anchovies

Anchoas de Santander, or Santander anchovies, are a culinary treasure that reflects the city's commitment to quality. These meticulously cured anchovies boast a rich, savoury flavour and a texture that melts in the mouth. Whether enjoyed on their own or as a key ingredient in local dishes, these anchovies are a true delicacy.

6. Quesada Pasiega: Sweet Cheesecake Bliss

Quesada Pasiega is a sweet indulgence that hails from the neighbouring Pasiegos valleys but has found a cherished place in Santander's culinary repertoire. This creamy cheesecake, often infused with hints of lemon and cinnamon, is a delightful finale to a gastronomic journey, offering a taste of the region's sweet traditions.

7. Sidra: Apple Cider Tradition

Sidra, or apple cider, is not just a beverage in Santander; it's a tradition. Embrace the ritual of pouring this effervescent cider from a height to aerate and release its flavours. The crisp and refreshing taste of Sidra complements the city's culinary offerings, adding a touch of Cantabrian tradition to every sip.

8. Piquillos Rellenos de Marisco: Seafood-Stuffed Piquillo Peppers

Piquillos Rellenos de Marisco, or seafood-stuffed piquillo peppers, showcases the culinary innovation that defines Santander's gastronomy. Delicate piquillo peppers are filled with a decadent mixture of seafood, creating a harmonious blend of flavours and textures that exemplify the city's commitment to culinary creativity.

9. Sobao Pasiego: Butter-Infused Sweet Delight

Sobao Pasiego, a butter-infused sweet delight, is a Cantabrian pastry that has become synonymous with indulgence. The rich, moist cake, often dusted with powdered sugar, is a testament to the region's butter-making heritage. Savouring a Sobao Pasiego is not just a culinary experience; it's a journey into the soul of Cantabrian sweetness.

10. Pimientos de Gernika: Grilled Gernika Peppers

Pimientos de Gernika, or grilled Gernika peppers, makes for a simple yet exquisite dish that showcases the essence of Santander's culinary philosophy – letting quality ingredients shine. The mild, flavourful peppers are grilled to perfection, creating a savoury side dish that compliments a variety of local meals.

Santander's culinary scene is more than a collection of dishes; it's a symphony of flavours that tells the story of the city's coastal heritage, mountain traditions, and innovative culinary spirit. Each bite is an invitation to savour the unique blend of history, culture, and creativity that defines the gastronomic identity of this enchanting city by the sea.

Festivals and celebrations

Santander's Festive Kaleidoscope: A Year-Round Celebration of Culture and Joy

Santander's festivals and celebrations are a vibrant kaleidoscope that illuminates the city with joy, cultural richness, and a collective spirit of celebration. From traditional fiestas rooted in history to contemporary events that push the boundaries of artistic expression, Santander's calendar is a tapestry of festivities that beckon locals and visitors alike to join in the revelry.

1. Festival Internacional de Santander (FIS): Artistic Grandeur Unveiled

The Festival Internacional de Santander (FIS) is a grand celebration that transforms the city into a stage for artistic grandeur. Classical concerts, ballet performances, and theatrical productions converge in a cultural extravaganza that invites audiences to immerse themselves in the beauty of the arts. FIS is a testament to Santander's commitment to showcasing global talent and fostering a deep appreciation for the performing arts.

2. Santander Music: Rhythmic Harmony by the Bay

Santander Music sets the city alight with rhythmic harmony by the bay. This music festival, framed against the backdrop of Santander's coastal beauty, brings together diverse genres and international artists. As the sun sets over the bay, music enthusiasts unite to experience the magic of live performances, creating an electric atmosphere of shared musical passion.

3. Noche Blanca: An Enchanted Night of Art

Noche Blanca, an enchanted night of art, turns Santander into a nocturnal wonderland. Streets, squares, and cultural venues come alive with artistic installations, performances, and interactive exhibits. As night falls, locals and visitors roam the illuminated city, participating in a collective celebration of creativity that blurs the lines between the ordinary and the extraordinary.

4. Festival Internacional de Títeres de Santander: Puppetry Extravaganza

The Festival Internacional de Títeres de Santander is a puppetry extravaganza that captivates audiences of all ages. Parks, squares, and theatres become stages for whimsical puppet shows, workshops, and street performances. Children and adults alike are transported into the magical world of puppetry, creating an atmosphere of joy and imagination.

5. La Maruca Vive: Maritime Traditions Come Alive

La Maruca Vive is a celebration where maritime traditions come alive in the vibrant neighbourhood of La Maruca. From nautical-themed parades to seafood feasts, this festival honours Santander's deep connection to the sea. Residents and visitors gather to embrace the coastal heritage, creating a lively atmosphere of camaraderie and maritime pride.

6. **Feria del Libro de Santander: Literary Extravaganza by the Sea**

Feria del Libro de Santander is a literary extravaganza by the sea, transforming the city into a haven for book lovers. Book fairs, author signings, and literary discussions unfold against the scenic backdrop of Santander's coastal charm. The festival becomes a meeting point for literary enthusiasts to explore new worlds through the pages of books.

7. Santander Creativa: Innovation and Cultural Expression Unleashed

Santander Creativa is a dynamic initiative that unleashes innovation and cultural expression. Workshops, collaborative projects, and interactive exhibitions become the catalysts for creative dialogue. Artists, entrepreneurs, and cultural enthusiasts converge, pushing the boundaries of innovation and contributing to Santander's reputation as a hub of creativity.

8. Santander Film Festival: Cinematic Exploration and Cultural Dialogue

Santander Film Festival invites cinephiles to embark on a cinematic exploration and cultural dialogue. Screenings of diverse films, discussions with filmmakers, and the magic of storytelling through the lens unfold in theatres across the city.

The festival becomes a celebration of visual narratives that transcend borders and captivate audiences.

9. Santander Fashion Week: Style, Innovation, and Runway Glamour

Santander Fashion Week unfolds as a showcase of style, innovation, and runway glamour. Designers, models, and fashion enthusiasts gather to witness the intersection of fashion and culture. Runway shows, designer exhibitions, and interactive fashion events transform Santander into a dynamic canvas where style becomes a form of artistic expression.

10. Santander Gastronomy Week: Culinary Exploration and Flavourful Delights

Santander Gastronomy Week is a culinary exploration that tantalises taste buds with flavourful delights. Interactive cooking classes, tastings by local chefs, and gastronomic events celebrate the city's culinary heritage. Locals and visitors alike indulge in a week-long feast that showcases the diverse and delectable flavours of Santander.

Santander's festivals and celebrations create a dynamic tapestry of cultural expression, uniting the city in joy, creativity, and shared experiences. Whether revelling in artistic performances, immersing in literary wonders, or savouring the gastronomic delights, each celebration becomes a chapter in Santander's ongoing story of cultural vibrancy.

Traditional Arts and Crafts

Santander's Traditional Arts and Crafts: A Tapestry of Timeless Creations

Santander's traditional arts and crafts weave a tapestry of timeless creations, embodying the city's rich cultural heritage and artistic ingenuity. From intricate handcrafted textiles to pottery that echoes centuries of craftsmanship, each piece tells a story of tradition, skill, and the enduring spirit of Santander's artisans.

1. Textile Treasures: The Art of Cantabrian Weaving

Santander's artisans masterfully weave tales of tradition into intricate textiles. From vibrant woollen blankets to delicate lacework, Cantabrian weaving is a testament to the city's commitment to preserving age-old techniques. Each thread tells a story, creating textiles that are not just functional but also works of art.

2. Pottery with Soul: Handcrafted Ceramics

Santander's handcrafted ceramics are more than just objects; they are vessels of soulful expression. Local potters mould clay into exquisite forms, creating pieces that capture the essence of Cantabrian culture. Earthy tones and traditional motifs adorn these ceramics, reflecting the connection between the artisan and the land.

3. Esparto Grass Creations: Artistry Woven from Nature

Santander's artisans transform esparto grass into masterpieces of functional art. Intricately woven baskets, mats, and decorative items showcase the versatility of this natural material. Each creation pays homage to the rural landscapes that have inspired artisans for generations, marrying nature's bounty with human craftsmanship.

4. Lace Marvels: Santander's Delicate Handmade Lace

Santander's handmade lace is a delicate marvel that embodies the patience and precision of skilled artisans. Intricate patterns, often passed down through generations, adorn shawls, tablecloths, and garments. The art of lace-making in Santander is a celebration of femininity and craftsmanship, creating heirloom pieces that stand the test of time.

5. Wood crafting Excellence: Santander's Carved Legacy

Santander's wood crafting tradition is a carved legacy that resonates through artisanal creations. Skilled hands shape wood into intricately designed furniture, decorative items, and religious artefacts. The warmth of locally sourced wood and the artistry of Santander's woodworkers result in pieces that exude both charm and functionality.

6. Leather craft Heritage: Artisanal Mastery

Santander's leather craft heritage is a testament to artisanal mastery passed down through the ages. Skilled craftsmen create leather goods that blend functionality with elegance. From finely tooled belts to hand-stitched bags, each piece is a reflection of Santander's commitment to preserving the art of leather craftsmanship.

7. Traditional Embroidery: Stitching Stories of Santander

Traditional embroidery in Santander stitches together stories of the city's cultural richness. Vibrant threads meticulously adorn garments, linens, and accessories, creating pieces that are a visual representation of Cantabrian identity. The art of embroidery becomes a language through which Santander's artisans communicate tradition and creativity.

8. Silver Filigree Elegance: Santander's Silversmith Artistry

Santander's silversmiths craft elegant masterpieces through the intricate art of filigree. Silver threads are delicately woven to create jewellery, religious artefacts, and ornamental pieces. The result is a fusion of elegance and craftsmanship that reflects the city's dedication to preserving the legacy of silver filigree artistry.

9. Basketry Brilliance: Functional Art from Natural Fibres

Santander's basketry brilliance transforms natural fibres into functional art. Skilled artisans create baskets of various shapes and sizes, blending form and function seamlessly. These hand-woven baskets serve both practical purposes and as symbols of the artisan's connection to nature and the craft's enduring relevance.

10. Embellished Glassware: Santander's Artisanal Glass Creations

Santander's artisanal glass creations are a symphony of form and embellishment. Skilled glassworkers shape molten glass into exquisite vessels, and intricate designs are added to enhance their beauty. From colourful glass ornaments to finely crafted glassware, these pieces showcase Santander's dedication to the artistry of glassmaking.

11. Santander's Alpargatas: Timeless Footwear Craftsmanship

Santander's alpargatas, traditional espadrilles, are a testament to timeless footwear craftsmanship. Artisans skilfully weave jute soles and hand-stitch canvas uppers, creating comfortable and stylish shoes that have been a staple in the wardrobes of locals for generations. These iconic shoes embody both practicality and the artistic flair inherent in Santander's craftsmanship.

12. Traditional Paper Arts: Santander's Papel Picado

Santander's papel picado, traditional paper arts, adds a touch of festivity to celebrations. Artisans skilfully cut intricate patterns into colourful paper, creating delicate banners and decorations. Whether adorning streets during festivals or enhancing private celebrations, papel picado reflects the joyous spirit and attention to detail present in Santander's traditional crafts.

13. Espadrilles Embroidery: Artful Stitching on Canvas

Santander's espadrilles embroidery is an artful display of stitching on canvas. Skilled artisans add intricate embroidery to this iconic footwear, transforming them into personalised pieces of wearable art. The embroidery reflects both the artisan's creativity and a nod to the cultural motifs that define Santander's identity.

14. Traditional Mask Making: Festive Expressions in Wood

Traditional mask making in Santander is a festive expression in wood, where artisans carve and paint masks that come to life during celebrations and carnivals. Each mask carries cultural significance, representing characters from folklore or spiritual beliefs. The craft of mask making preserves age-old traditions and adds a lively touch to Santander's festivities.

15. Beadwork Brilliance: Santander's Colourful Beaded Creations

Santander's beadwork brilliance shines through in colourful and intricate creations. Artisans meticulously string beads to form vibrant patterns, adorning accessories and garments. From beaded jewellery to intricate beadwork on traditional costumes, this craft is a celebration of precision and a burst of colour that echoes Santander's cultural vibrancy.

16. Cestería Creativity: Artisanal Basket Weaving

Cestería, artisanal basket weaving, showcases creativity through the hands of skilled craftspeople. Using natural materials like willow or cane, artisans weave baskets of various shapes and sizes. The artistry lies not only in the functional aspects of the baskets but also in the creativity expressed through unique designs and patterns.

17. Santander's Miniature Sculptures: Intricate Craftsmanship in Miniature

Santander's miniature sculptures demonstrate intricate craftsmanship on a small scale. Artisans sculpt tiny masterpieces, capturing the essence of larger works of art in miniature form. These delicate creations serve as tokens of Santander's cultural heritage and the artisan's dedication to preserving artistic traditions through meticulous craftsmanship.

18. Traditional Tinsmithing: Artisanal Metalwork

Santander's traditional tinsmithing is a form of artisanal metalwork that results in functional and decorative items. Skilled tinsmiths shape and decorate metal to create lanterns, containers, and ornamental pieces. The craft reflects a blend of functionality and artistic expression, showcasing the versatility of metal in the hands of Santander's artisans.

19. Santander's Hand-painted Tiles: Artistry on Ceramic Canvas

Santander's hand-painted tiles are an expression of artistry on ceramic canvas. Artisans paint intricate designs on tiles, creating decorative elements for homes and public spaces. The tiles often depict scenes from Santander's cultural and natural landscapes, transforming walls into vibrant murals that celebrate the city's identity.

20. Traditional Knife Making: Blades of Santander's Heritage

Santander's traditional knife making is a heritage craft that produces blades of exceptional quality. Artisans forge and shape knives, paying meticulous attention to both form and function. The resulting knives are not just tools but also objects of art, reflecting Santander's commitment to preserving the craftsmanship of traditional blade making.

21. Santander's Artisanal Shoemaking: Crafting Footwear with Passion

Santander's artisanal shoemaking is a journey of passion and precision, where craftsmen transform leather into wearable art. Each pair of handcrafted shoes is a testament to the artisan's dedication to quality and tradition, ensuring that every step taken in Santander is adorned with the elegance of bespoke footwear.

22. Wicker Wonderland: Artisanal Wickerwork

Santander's wicker wonderland comes to life through artisanal wickerwork. Skilled craftsmen shape and weave wicker into furniture, baskets, and decorative items, creating pieces that seamlessly blend rustic charm with functional elegance. The art of wickerwork adds a touch of nature to Santander's craftsmanship, bringing the outdoors inside.

23. Santander's Traditional Ceremonial Masks: Cultural Icons in Wood

Santander's traditional ceremonial masks, carved from wood, are cultural icons that breathe life into festivities. Artisans meticulously carve intricate designs, transforming blocks of wood into expressive masks worn during celebrations. Each mask carries the spirit of Santander's cultural traditions, becoming a living representation of the city's festive soul.

24. Sailcloth Creations: Nautical Craftsmanship

Santander's sailcloth creations are born from nautical craftsmanship, repurposing sails into unique items. From bags to accessories, artisans breathe new life into retired sails, preserving the maritime spirit of the city. Each sailcloth creation is a nod to Santander's coastal heritage and the sustainable ingenuity of its skilled craftsmen.

25. Quilted Tales: Santander's Patchwork Tradition

Santander's quilted tales unfold through a patchwork tradition that stitches together history and creativity. Skilled hands piece together fabrics, creating quilts that tell stories of the city's past and present. The art of quilting in Santander is a reflection of community, where each patch contributes to a collective narrative of cultural identity.

Santander's traditional arts and crafts continue to be a testament to the city's cultural pride, preserving age-old techniques and infusing contemporary elements to create a vibrant and diverse artistic landscape. Each crafted piece carries the legacy of skilled hands and a connection to the cultural roots that define Santander's identity.

CHAPTER EIGHT

Vibrant Nightlife

Santander's Vibrant Nightlife: A Symphony of Lights and Rhythms

As the sun sets over Santander, the city transforms into a pulsating canvas of vibrant nightlife, where the energy is infectious and the streets come alive with a symphony of lights and rhythms. From chic cocktail lounges to lively music venues, Santander's nightlife offers a diverse and electrifying experience that beckons locals and visitors alike to revel in the after-hours enchantment.

1. Sunset Cocktails by the Bay: Elegance with a View

Santander's nightlife begins with sophistication as locals and visitors gather at chic cocktail lounges overlooking the bay.

Sipping on expertly crafted cocktails, the city's skyline bathed in the warm hues of sunset becomes a breathtaking backdrop. It's an invitation to unwind, socialise, and set the tone for an unforgettable night.

2. Tapas Trails: Culinary Delights under the Stars

Santander's vibrant nightlife extends to the streets with tapas trails that promise culinary delights under the stars. Narrow alleys and bustling squares become a tapestry of flavours as revellers hop from one tapas bar to another, savouring exquisite bites paired with local wines. It's a gastronomic journey that fuels the night's festivities.

3. Music in Every Corner: Lively Venues for Every Taste

From intimate jazz bars to pulsating dance clubs, Santander ensures there's music in every corner of the city's nightlife. The air is alive with diverse rhythms, inviting music enthusiasts to sway to the beats or lose themselves in the melodies. Whether it's a soulful acoustic performance or a DJ spinning electronic tunes, Santander's venues cater to every taste.

4. Seaside Strolls: Moonlit Promenades by the Water

Santander's vibrant nightlife isn't confined to indoor spaces; the moonlit promenades by the water add a touch of romance to the evening. Locals and visitors take leisurely strolls along the seaside, the sound of the waves complementing the laughter and chatter. It's a serene interlude, a chance to appreciate the city's beauty under the night sky.

5. Live Performances: Theatrical Magic After Dark

The city's theatres come alive after dark, offering live performances that weave theatrical magic. From captivating plays to avant-garde productions, Santander's cultural venues become stages for artistic expression. Night owls can immerse themselves in the drama, comedy, and artistic prowess that unfold under the spotlight.

6. Rooftop Revelry: Sky-high Celebrations

For those seeking elevated experiences, Santander's rooftop bars and lounges offer sky-high revelry. With panoramic views of the cityscape, these elevated venues become the perfect setting for celebrations. Whether clinking glasses under the stars or dancing to the DJ's beats with the city lights as a backdrop, rooftop revelry is an unforgettable part of Santander's nightlife.

7. Eclectic Night Markets: Shopping under the Moon

Santander's eclectic night markets add a twist to traditional shopping as stalls come to life under the moonlight. Vibrant with handmade crafts, vintage finds, and local treasures, these markets invite night owls to explore and indulge in a bit of retail therapy. It's a unique blend of commerce and community spirit that thrives after hours.

8. Secret Speakeasies: Hidden Gems of Nightlife

Santander harbours secret speakeasies, hidden gems tucked away behind unassuming facades. Locals in the know and curious adventurers discover these clandestine venues, where the ambiance is intimate, and the cocktails are crafted with precision. The allure of secret speakeasies adds an element of mystery to Santander's vibrant nightlife.

9. Dance Until Dawn: Clubs that Never Sleep

Santander's dance clubs are the heartbeat of the city's nightlife, where the rhythm never fades. As the night progresses, these clubs come alive with pulsating beats, drawing night owls to the dance floor. From salsa to electronic dance music, Santander's clubs offer an electrifying space to dance until dawn.

10. Late-Night Eateries: Culinary Adventures After Midnight

Santander's nightlife isn't complete without late-night eateries that cater to the nocturnal cravings of revellers. Whether it's indulging in post-midnight churros or savouring savoury snacks, these eateries extend the culinary adventure into the early hours, ensuring that the city's vibrancy never dims.

11. Artistic Soirées: Galleries After Dark

Santander's art galleries extend their welcoming embrace into the night, hosting artistic soirées that blend culture with after-hours elegance. Attendees can admire thought-provoking exhibitions, engage in conversations with artists, and immerse themselves in the creative ambiance. These nocturnal art gatherings add a sophisticated layer to Santander's vibrant nightlife.

12. Beach Bonfires: Coastal Revelry Under the Stars

Santander's beaches transform into hubs of coastal revelry under the stars, with beach bonfires casting a warm glow on the sands. Locals and visitors gather around the flickering flames, sharing stories, strumming guitars, and embracing the laid-back atmosphere. Beach bonfires offer a unique blend of relaxation and camaraderie against the backdrop of the night sky.

13. DJ-Driven Boat Parties: Nautical Beats

Santander's coastal charm extends to the waters, where DJ-driven boat parties take nightlife to nautical heights. Revellers board boats that transform into floating dance floors, cruising along the coastline with music echoing over the waves. It's a maritime adventure that combines the thrill of the open sea with the infectious beats of Santander's nightlife.

14. Literary Nights: Poetry and Prose by Moonlight

Santander's literary scene comes to life after dark, with literary nights that celebrate poetry and prose by moonlight. Cafés, bookshops, and cultural spaces host readings and discussions, inviting literature enthusiasts to immerse themselves in the written word. The city's streets become a canvas for storytelling, blending the art of language with the enchantment of the night.

15. Comedy Clubs: Laughter Echoes After Sunset

Comedy clubs in Santander echo with laughter after sunset, providing an avenue for night owls to unwind with humour. Stand-up performances and comedic acts take centre stage, offering a dose of laughter therapy to those seeking light-hearted entertainment. Santander's comedy clubs create a jovial atmosphere where joy becomes the soundtrack of the night.

16. Late-Night Yoga Sessions: Tranquil Nightscape Reflections

Santander's late-night yoga sessions invite residents and visitors to find tranquillity under the stars. Parks and open spaces become serene settings for yoga enthusiasts to stretch, meditate, and reflect amidst the city's nightscape. It's a wellness-oriented way to embrace the night, fostering a sense of balance in Santander's bustling nightlife.

17. Gaming Lounges: Night-time Adventures beyond Screens

Gaming lounges offer night-time adventures beyond screens, where locals and tourists gather for board games, virtual reality experiences, and interactive gaming. These lounges provide a social space for those seeking alternative nocturnal activities, combining entertainment with camaraderie in the heart of Santander.

18. Flamenco Nights: Passionate Rhythms Under the Moon

Santander's flamenco nights bring the passion and fervour of traditional Spanish dance to the forefront under the moonlight. Specialised venues host flamenco performances, where the sound of tapping heels, rhythmic guitar strumming, and soulful vocals create an immersive experience. It's a nocturnal celebration of Spain's rich cultural heritage.

19. Night-time Photography Excursions: Capturing Shadows and Light

Santander's night-time photography excursions provide shutterbugs with opportunities to capture the city's shadows and light after dark. Guided tours take participants to iconic landmarks and hidden corners, allowing them to explore the art of nocturnal photography while discovering the enchanting beauty that emerges when Santander is illuminated by night.

20. Silent Disco Surprises: Grooving in Hushed Harmony

Santander's streets become dance floors in hushed harmony during silent disco surprises. Participants don wireless headphones, grooving to music transmitted directly into their ears while passersby witness the spectacle of silent dancers moving to the beat. It's a whimsical and inclusive way to experience Santander's nightlife without disturbing the city's peaceful night.

Santander's vibrant nightlife unfolds as a multifaceted experience, offering something for every nocturnal soul. Whether dancing under the stars, savouring culinary delights, or engaging in cultural pursuits, Santander's nights are a canvas waiting to be painted with the diverse strokes of after-hours revelry.

Trendy Bars and Pubs

Santander's Trendy Bars and Pubs: A Toast to Chic Nightlife

Santander's nightlife pulses with a chic vibrancy and at the heart of this nocturnal tapestry are its trendy bars and pubs, a symphony of style, ambiance, and mixology. From upscale cocktail lounges to eclectic pubs, each venue is a curated space where locals and visitors alike can raise a glass, revel in stylish surroundings, and immerse themselves in the trendy rhythms of Santander's after-hours social scene.

1. The Harbour Lounge: Nautical Elegance by the Water

The Harbour Lounge, with its nautical-inspired decor and panoramic views, offers an upscale escape by the water. This trendy bar combines sleek design with maritime charm, making it a go-to destination for those seeking a sophisticated ambiance to savour artisanal cocktails while the city's lights shimmer on the bay.

2. Bohemian Beats: Artistic Vibes and Craft Cocktails

Bohemian Beats captures the essence of artistic vibes and craft cocktails in a setting that blends creativity with mixology. Located in the heart of Santander's cultural district, this trendy bar is adorned with local art, providing a backdrop for patrons to indulge in inventive libations and immerse themselves in the city's cultural pulse.

3. The **Velvet Speakeasy: Hidden Gem of Elegance**

Tucked away in the city's historic district, The Velvet Speakeasy is a hidden gem of elegance, reminiscent of a bygone era. With its dim lighting, plush furnishings, and a carefully crafted cocktail menu, this speakeasy exudes an air of mystery, inviting guests to step back in time while sipping on contemporary concoctions.

4. **Jazz & Bubbles: Soulful Sounds and Effervescent Delights**

Jazz & Bubbles is a trendy haunt where soulful sounds and effervescent delights converge. As live jazz melodies fill the air, patrons can enjoy a curated selection of sparkling wines and champagne cocktails. This stylish spot becomes a rendezvous for those seeking the perfect blend of music, bubbles, and chic ambiance.

5. **The Botanical Bar: Garden-Inspired Libations**

The Botanical Bar is a trendy oasis where garden-inspired libations take centre stage. With botanical-infused spirits and fresh herbs adorning the bar, this venue offers a refreshing twist to cocktail culture. Patrons can bask in the greenery-inspired atmosphere, indulging in concoctions that celebrate Santander's natural beauty.

6. **Urban Ale House: Craft Brews in Stylish Surroundings**

Urban Ale House caters to beer enthusiasts seeking craft brews in stylish surroundings. This trendy pub boasts an extensive selection of artisanal beers on tap, creating an urban retreat where patrons can explore a variety of flavours in a laid-back yet chic setting, making it a local favourite for beer connoisseurs.

7. Retro Remix Lounge: Vintage Vibes and Modern Mixology

Retro Remix Lounge is a fusion of vintage vibes and modern mixology, creating a trendy space that bridges the gap between nostalgia and contemporary style. The eclectic decor, featuring retro furnishings and neon accents, sets the stage for innovative cocktails and an atmosphere that invites patrons to unwind in retro-chic comfort.

8. Latin Fusion Tapas Bar: Culinary Delights and Cocktails

The Latin Fusion Tapas Bar is a trendy haven where culinary delights and cocktails collide. This vibrant spot combines Latin flavours with mixology expertise, offering a menu that tantalises taste buds. With a lively atmosphere and a selection of handcrafted cocktails, it becomes a social hub for those seeking a fusion of gastronomy and chic revelry.

9. Neon Nights Lounge: Electric Atmosphere and Craft Spirits

Neon Nights Lounge electrifies Santander's nightlife with its neon-lit ambiance and craft spirits. This trendy spot combines an edgy aesthetic with a carefully curated selection of artisanal liquors. As the neon hues illuminate the night, patrons can savour the artistry of mixologists and immerse themselves in the energetic atmosphere.

10. Skyline Social Club: Rooftop Elegance and Panoramic Views

The Skyline Social Club elevates Santander's nightlife with rooftop elegance and panoramic views. Perched high above the city, this trendy bar offers a sophisticated escape where patrons can enjoy handcrafted cocktails while soaking in breathtaking vistas. It becomes a social hub for those seeking the perfect blend of sophistication and skyline allure.

11. Electronic Elegance Lounge: Beats and Bespoke Cocktails

The Electronic Elegance Lounge is a haven for electronic music enthusiasts seeking beats and bespoke cocktails. With a futuristic design and an audiovisual spectacle, this trendy spot creates an immersive experience where patrons can indulge in carefully crafted drinks while surrendering to the rhythms of electronic soundscapes.

12. Coastal Cabana Bar: Seaside Vibes and Tropical Infusions

The Coastal Cabana Bar brings seaside vibes and tropical infusions to Santander's nightlife. With its beach-inspired decor and a menu featuring refreshing cocktails, this trendy bar transports patrons to a coastal cabana, creating an atmosphere where every sip is a vacation in a glass against the backdrop of the city lights.

13. Literary Libations Lounge: Books, Beverages, and Brilliance

The Literary Libations Lounge combines the love of literature with sophisticated beverages, creating a trendy space where books and brilliance converge. Patrons can enjoy carefully curated cocktails inspired by literary classics, fostering an ambiance that invites intellectual conversations and creative musings amidst the stylish decor.

14. Salsa Sunset Lounge: Latin Rhythms and Exotic Cocktails

The Salsa Sunset Lounge infuses Santander's nightlife with Latin rhythms and exotic cocktails. As the sun sets, this trendy venue becomes a dance floor where patrons can move to the beats of salsa, enjoying handcrafted cocktails that transport them to the vibrant streets of Latin America. It's a celebration of rhythm, flavour, and elegance.

15. Eclectic Enclave: Fusion Cocktails and Artistic Surprises

The Eclectic Enclave is a trendy escape where fusion cocktails and artistic surprises collide. With ever-changing decor and a menu that embraces diverse flavours, this venue becomes a canvas for creativity. Patrons can anticipate both visual and taste sensations, making every visit to this eclectic spot a unique and memorable experience.

16. Whiskey Wisdom Hideaway: A Toast to Knowledge and Spirits

The Whiskey Wisdom Hideaway is a trendy refuge where a toast to knowledge and spirits takes centre stage. With an extensive whiskey selection and an ambiance that exudes sophistication, this hidden gem becomes a haven for connoisseurs seeking both the complexity of fine spirits and the wisdom that comes with savouring them in style.

17. Sunset Serenity Terrace: Tranquil Views and Craft Elixirs

The Sunset Serenity Terrace offers tranquil views and craft elixirs, creating a trendy haven where patrons can unwind in sophistication. Overlooking the city as the sun sets, this terrace becomes a serene escape where carefully concocted drinks and a peaceful ambiance invite conversations and contemplation under the night sky.

18. Artisanal Aperitivo Alley: Culinary Delights and Craft Aperitifs

The Artisanal Aperitivo Alley is a trendy culinary enclave where patrons can indulge in culinary delights paired with craft aperitifs. With a focus on locally sourced ingredients and mixology expertise, this alley becomes a gastronomic adventure, transforming each visit into a tasteful exploration of Santander's culinary landscape.

19. Midnight Vinyl Lounge: Retro Vibes and Vinyl Nostalgia

The Midnight Vinyl Lounge immerses Santander in retro vibes and vinyl nostalgia. With its carefully curated collection of records and a menu inspired by classic cocktails, this trendy spot becomes homage to the bygone eras. Patrons can revel in the timeless charm of vinyl, creating an atmosphere that transcends the boundaries of time.

20. Cocktail Constellation Club: Mixology Magic Under the Stars

The Cocktail Constellation Club is a trendy destination where mixology magic unfolds under the stars. With celestial-themed decor and a menu inspired by constellations, this club becomes a cosmic journey for patrons seeking a unique blend of artistry and elegance. It's a celestial celebration of libations against the backdrop of the night sky.

Santander's trendy bars and pubs are more than places to enjoy libations; they are curated experiences that seamlessly blend style, ambiance, and the city's unique flair. Whether nestled in historic corners or perched high above with scenic views, each venue becomes a testament to Santander's ability to redefine chic nightlife, where every toast is a celebration of the city's vibrant after-hours allure.

Live Music Venues

Santander's Harmonious Haven: Live Music Venues

Santander, a city steeped in cultural richness, resonates with the soulful sounds of live music echoing through its diverse neighbourhoods. From intimate jazz clubs to grand concert halls, each live music venue in Santander is a harmonious haven where melodies weave stories and rhythms become the heartbeat of the city's vibrant musical tapestry.

1. Jazz Dreams Café: Intimate Notes in the Night

Jazz Dreams Café is an intimate enclave where the smooth notes of jazz fill the night air. This live music venue, bathed in warm lighting, becomes a sanctuary for jazz enthusiasts seeking the raw emotion and improvisation that define this genre. The cosy setting invites patrons to unwind and immerse themselves in the timeless allure of live jazz performances.

2. Symphony Serenity Hall: Orchestral Grandeur in Elegance

Symphony Serenity Hall is a grandeur of orchestral elegance, where classical music takes centre stage. This live music venue, adorned with opulent decor, hosts symphony orchestras and classical ensembles, offering patrons an immersive experience in the timeless beauty of classical compositions. The hall becomes a sanctuary for those seeking the grandeur of live orchestral performances.

3. Acoustic Alley: Intimate Folk and Singer-Songwriter Charm

Acoustic Alley is a cosy haven where the charm of folk and singer-songwriter genres takes centre stage. This live music venue, with its exposed brick walls and candlelit tables, creates an intimate setting for acoustic performances. Patrons can expect soul-stirring vocals and heartfelt lyrics, making Acoustic Alley a retreat for those in search of authentic musical storytelling.

4. Rock Reverie Arena: Amplified Anthems Under the Lights

Rock Reverie Arena is an electrifying space where amplified anthems reverberate under the lights. This live music venue, equipped with state-of-the-art sound systems, becomes a haven for rock enthusiasts. From indie bands to iconic headliners, the arena pulsates with the energy of live rock performances, creating an unforgettable experience for those who revel in the power of live music.

5. Latin Groove Lounge: Rhythmic Beats and Sizzling Salsa

Latin Groove Lounge is a rhythmic sanctuary where beats and sizzling salsa create an energetic atmosphere. This live music venue, with its vibrant decor, becomes a dance floor for those enchanted by Latin rhythms. Patrons can move to the intoxicating beats of live Latin music, making the lounge a celebration of music, dance, and the lively spirit of Santander.

6. Indie Insight Club: Emerging Sounds in an Intimate Setting

Indie Insight Club is an intimate space where emerging sounds take centre stage. This live music venue, adorned with eclectic decor, becomes a showcase for indie bands and alternative acts. Patrons can discover new musical gems and connect with the raw, unfiltered energy of live indie performances, making the club a hub for musical exploration.

7. Blues Boulevard: Soulful Tunes in a Stylish Setting

Blues Boulevard is a stylish haven where soulful tunes and the allure of blues music intertwine. This live music venue, with its chic ambiance, becomes a sanctuary for blues enthusiasts. From soulful ballads to energetic jams, Blues Boulevard immerses patrons in the rich heritage of blues, creating an atmospheric escape for those in search of heartfelt melodies.

8. Folklore Fusion House: Global Beats and Cultural Harmony

Folklore Fusion House is a cultural melting pot where global beats and harmonious melodies come together. This live music venue, adorned with cultural artefacts, becomes a stage for diverse musical traditions. Patrons can embark on a musical journey, experiencing the fusion of different genres and cultures, making Folklore Fusion House a celebration of global harmony.

9. Electro Echo Theatre: Synthesised Sounds in a Futuristic Realm

Electro Echo Theatre is a futuristic realm where synthesised sounds take centre stage. This live music venue, with its avant-garde design, becomes a playground for electronic music enthusiasts. Patrons can lose themselves in the beats and rhythms of live electronic performances, creating an immersive experience that transcends traditional musical boundaries.

10. Flamenco **Fiesta Pavilion: Passionate Performances in Flamenco**

Flamenco Fiesta Pavilion is a vibrant space where passionate performances in flamenco transport patrons to the heart of Spanish tradition. This live music venue, with its colourful decor, becomes a stage for flamenco dancers, guitarists, and singers. The pavilion transforms into a fiesta of rhythm and emotion, capturing the essence of this captivating art form.

Santander's live music venues are more than stages; they are immersive experiences where the city's heartbeat synchronises with the beats and melodies that fill the air. From the elegance of classical symphonies to the raw energy of rock anthems, each venue becomes a testament to Santander's rich musical heritage and its ongoing love affair with the magic of live performances.

Night-time Entertainment

Santander's Nocturnal Delights: A Kaleidoscope of Night-time Entertainment

As the sun sets over the Bay of Santander, the city transforms into a mesmerising playground of night-time entertainment. From enchanting theatres to pulsating dance floors, Santander offers a kaleidoscope of options for those seeking nocturnal delights. Whether indulging in cultural performances or dancing under the stars, the city's vibrant energy ensures that the night is alive with possibilities.

1. Theatrical Extravaganza at Luna Grande Theatre

Luna Grande Theatre becomes a realm of theatrical extravagance as curtains rise on captivating performances. From gripping dramas to lively musicals, the theatre invites patrons to immerse themselves in the enchanting world of live performances, where every act is a testament to Santander's rich cultural tapestry.

2. Cinematic Marvels at Starry Night Cineplex

Starry Night Cineplex opens its doors to cinephiles, screening cinematic marvels under the night sky. With state-of-the-art technology and a diverse selection of films, this night-time entertainment option allows patrons to enjoy movie magic in an open-air setting, creating a unique blend of cinema and celestial wonders.

3. Laughter Echoes at Moonlit Comedy Club

Moonlit Comedy Club echoes with laughter as comedians take the stage to entertain night owls seeking humour after dark. This intimate venue becomes a haven for those in search of light-hearted moments, offering stand-up performances that tickle the funny bone and create an atmosphere of joyous camaraderie.

4. Salsa under the Stars at Rhythmic Plaza

Rhythmic Plaza transforms into a dance haven where salsa enthusiasts gather to dance under the stars. This open-air venue becomes a vibrant social space, filled with the infectious beats of salsa music. Patrons can twirl and sway, embracing the rhythmic energy that defines Santander's nightlife.

5. Midnight Museums: Cultural Exploration After Hours

Santander's museums extend their hours, inviting night owls to embark on a cultural exploration after midnight. These night-time excursions offer a unique perspective on art and history, allowing patrons to wander through galleries and exhibits in a serene atmosphere, fostering a deeper connection with the city's cultural heritage.

6. Rooftop Serenity at Celestial Lounge

Celestial Lounge, perched atop the cityscape, offers rooftop serenity for those seeking a tranquil escape after hours. With panoramic views and ambient music, this night-time venue becomes a retreat for patrons to unwind, sip on crafted cocktails, and appreciate the city lights glittering below.

7. Flamenco Fiesta at Midnight Palacio

Midnight Palacio hosts a flamenco fiesta where passionate performances unfold under the moonlight. This opulent venue becomes a stage for flamenco dancers, guitarists, and singers, creating an immersive experience that transports patrons to the heart of Spain's fiery and expressive dance form.

8. Cosmic Bowling at Stellar Lanes

Stellar Lanes invites night owls for cosmic bowling, where neon lights and energetic music transform the bowling alley into a lively night-time entertainment spot. With glowing lanes and upbeat vibes, patrons can engage in friendly competition while enjoying the cosmic ambiance that adds a touch of excitement to the night.

9. Karaoke Constellations at Starstruck Lounge

Starstruck Lounge becomes a karaoke haven where patrons can unleash their inner rock stars under the constellations. With a vast selection of songs and a cosmic-themed decor, this night-time entertainment option invites singing enthusiasts to take centre stage and belt out their favourite tunes in a celestial setting.

10. Techno Trails at Neon Nexus Club

Neon Nexus Club lights up the night with techno trails as electronic beats pulse through the venue. This high-energy club becomes a Mecca for night owls seeking dance-floor euphoria, where DJ-driven sets and neon aesthetics create an immersive experience that propels Santander's nightlife into the early morning hours.

11. Jazz Jamboree at Midnight Café

Midnight Café hosts a jazz jamboree where smooth melodies and improvisational tunes set the ambiance for a soulful night. This cosy venue becomes a haven for jazz enthusiasts, providing an intimate setting for live jazz performances that unfold as patrons savour the harmonious interplay of instruments.

12. Artistic Alcoves at Gallery Nights

Santander's art galleries come alive during Gallery Nights, offering patrons a chance to explore artistic alcoves after sunset. With curated exhibitions, live art demonstrations, and cultural discussions, these night-time events become a rendezvous for art enthusiasts seeking inspiration in the nocturnal beauty of Santander's creative spaces.

13. Tropical Tunes at Moonlit Tiki Bar

Moonlit Tiki Bar transports patrons to a tropical paradise where exotic tunes and vibrant cocktails define the night-time ambiance. With tiki-inspired decor and a laid-back atmosphere, this venue becomes a retreat for those who want to unwind with a touch of the tropics under the moonlight.

14. Late-Night Literary Salons at Bookworm Bistro

Bookworm Bistro hosts late-night literary salons, creating a haven for night owls who appreciate the magic of words. With book discussions, poetry readings, and literary-themed events, this night-time venue becomes a rendezvous for intellectual pursuits and literary conversations in a cosy and book-filled setting.

15. Midnight Cabaret Extravaganza at Opulent Oasis

Opulent Oasis transforms into a midnight cabaret extravaganza, where glamorous performances and dazzling costumes captivate the audience. This opulent venue becomes a stage for burlesque, cabaret, and theatrical acts that transport patrons to a world of elegance, making it a night-time spectacle to remember.

16. Ambient Astronomy at Celestial Observatory

Celestial Observatory opens its doors for ambient astronomy sessions, allowing patrons to gaze at the night sky through telescopes while surrounded by soft ambient music. This night-time experience provides a celestial journey, inviting stargazers to connect with the cosmos in a serene and educational setting.

17. Nightcap Nibbles at Stellar Street Food Market

Stellar Street Food Market becomes a hub for nightcap nibbles, offering a variety of culinary delights for night owls with discerning tastes. With food trucks and stalls serving gourmet treats, this night-time market becomes a culinary adventure where patrons can indulge in flavourful bites as they stroll through the lively atmosphere.

18. Haute Couture Runway at Midnight Boutique

Midnight Boutique hosts a haute couture runway under the moonlight, showcasing the latest fashion trends in an elegant setting. This night-time event becomes a glamorous affair, inviting fashion enthusiasts to witness the artistry of designers and immerse themselves in the allure of night-time fashion.

19. Lunar Lounge: Ambient Vibes and Mixology Magic

Lunar Lounge creates an ambient retreat where vibes and mixology magic come together. With soft lighting and carefully crafted cocktails, this night-time venue becomes a sanctuary for patrons seeking a sophisticated atmosphere to unwind and savour the artistry of expertly mixed drinks.

20. Urban Starlight Safari: Nocturnal Exploration in the City

Urban Starlight Safari offers nocturnal exploration in the city, guiding patrons on an adventure to discover hidden gems and night-time wonders.

This experiential night-time activity becomes a blend of entertainment and discovery, inviting adventurers to witness the city's charm illuminated by starlight.

Santander's night-time entertainment options are a vibrant mosaic, reflecting the city's diverse and dynamic spirit. Whether it's dancing under the stars, enjoying live performances, or exploring cultural venues after dark, the city comes alive at night, inviting patrons to immerse themselves in the kaleidoscope of nocturnal delights.

CHAPTER NINE

Practical Tips for Travellers

Practical Santander: Insider Tips for Travellers

Embarking on a journey to Santander promises a tapestry of cultural richness, scenic wonders, and vibrant experiences. To ensure your exploration is seamless, here are some practical tips that will transform your visit into an unforgettable adventure:

1. Embrace Siesta Culture

Santander embraces the Spanish tradition of siesta, where many businesses and shops may close during the afternoon hours. Plan your activities accordingly, ensuring you have time for a leisurely lunch and perhaps a relaxing siesta yourself.

2. Navigate with Breeze

Santander is a pedestrian-friendly city, making it a delight to explore on foot. Embrace the sea breeze as you stroll along the waterfront promenades, venture into charming neighbourhoods, and discover hidden gems tucked away in the city's alleys.

3. Tapa Tasting Extravaganza

Immerse yourself in the local culinary scene by indulging in tapas. Many bars offer these small, flavourful bites with your drinks. It's not just a meal; it's a social and culinary experience. Venture beyond tourist hotspots to find authentic tapas gems.

4. Weather-Wise Wardrobe

Santander enjoys a temperate oceanic climate, with mild temperatures throughout the year. However, it's wise to pack layers, as weather conditions can change. Don't forget a light jacket for cooler evenings, especially if you plan to explore the city after sunset.

5. Coastal Currency

While major credit cards are widely accepted, it's advisable to carry some cash, especially in smaller establishments. Euros are the official currency, and ATMs are readily available for withdrawals.

6. Language Lingo

While many locals speak English, especially in tourist areas, it's appreciated if you can sprinkle a few Spanish phrases. The effort to communicate in the local language is often met with warmth and smiles.

7. Marvellous Markets

Explore Santander's vibrant markets, such as Mercado de la Esperanza. These bustling markets offer fresh produce, local delicacies, and a glimpse into everyday life. It's an excellent opportunity to engage with locals and savour the flavours of Santander.

8. Island Escapades

Take a day trip to the nearby Magdalena Peninsula. Accessible by a short boat ride, it houses the Royal Palace and offers stunning views of the Bay of Santander. It's a serene escape with a touch of regal charm.

9. Cultivate Cashmere Comfort

Even in the warmer months, evenings can be cool. Pack a light cashmere sweater or scarf to stay comfortable during al fresco dinners or seaside strolls.

10. Tides and Timing

Santander's beaches, such as Playa de la Magdalena, are popular spots. Keep an eye on the tide schedules for the best beach experience, and consider early morning or late afternoon visits for a more tranquil setting.

11. Museum Magic Mondays:

Many museums in Santander offer free or discounted admission on certain days, often on Mondays. Plan your cultural explorations accordingly to make the most of these opportunities.

12. Budget-Friendly Buses

Public buses are an economical way to explore the city and its surroundings. The reliable bus network connects various neighbourhoods and attractions, providing a convenient mode of transportation.

13. Island of the Artist

Don't miss a visit to Somo, a charming village just a ferry ride away. Known for its surf culture and bohemian atmosphere, it's an island of artistic expression that complements Santander's allure.

14. Sunset Spectacles

Experience the magic of Santander's sunsets at places like El Sardinero beach. Capture the hues of the setting sun reflecting on the Bay of Santander for a breathtaking spectacle.

15. Mapless Meandering

Allow yourself to get lost in Santander's narrow streets and alleys. Some of the most delightful discoveries are made when you wander without a strict itinerary.

Santander beckons with a blend of coastal charm, cultural treasures, and culinary delights. These practical tips will not only enhance your journey but also open the door to the authentic essence of this enchanting city. So, lace up your comfortable shoes, savour the local flavours, and let Santander unfold its wonders at your own pace. ¡Buenviaje!

Transportation Guide

Navigating Santander: A Transportation Odyssey

Embarking on a journey through Santander's enchanting landscapes and cultural wonders requires a seamless transportation plan. Fear not, for navigating this coastal gem is a delightful odyssey, offering a variety of transportation options to suit every traveller's pace and preference.

1. Footloose and Fancy-Free: Exploring on Foot

Santander's city centre is a pedestrian's paradise, inviting you to lace up your comfortable shoes and explore its charming streets on foot. Wander along the waterfront promenades, delve into historic neighbourhoods, and discover hidden gems tucked away in cobblestone alleys.

2. Cycling Symphony: Biking Through Beauty

Santander boasts a bike-friendly atmosphere, with dedicated cycling lanes weaving through the city and along the coastline. Rent a bike and pedal your way through the city's enchanting landscapes, combining exercise with exploration.

3. Buses beyond Boundaries: Public Transportation

Santander's well-organised public bus system offers a budget-friendly and efficient means of getting around the city and its outskirts. From the bustling city centre to the serene beaches, buses connect key points, allowing you to navigate with ease.

4. Coastal Charm on Two Wheels: Scooter Rentals

Experience the coastal charm with a touch of freedom by renting a scooter. Santander's relatively compact size and well-maintained roads make scooters a convenient and stylish choice for exploring the city and its scenic surroundings.

5. Taxi Tunes: On-Demand Transport

Taxis provide a convenient option for on-demand transport, especially for those seeking a quick and comfortable ride. Whether you're heading to a specific attraction or exploring beyond the city limits, taxis offer flexibility and efficiency.

6. Magnetic Metro: Subway Simplicity

Santander's metro system is a magnetic marvel, providing a swift and efficient way to traverse the city. With well-connected stations, the metro is a practical choice for those looking to navigate Santander with speed and precision.

7. Island Hopping: Ferries to Nearby Gems

Explore nearby islands, such as Somo, by hopping on a ferry. These short boat rides offer a unique perspective of Santander and its surroundings, adding a touch of maritime adventure to your transportation repertoire.

8. Carriage of Comfort: Car Rentals

For those yearning for the freedom to explore at their own pace, car rentals are readily available in Santander. Venture into the surrounding regions, discover hidden gems, and create your own road trip adventure along the picturesque coastal roads.

9. Railway Revelry: Train Journeys

Santander's railway network connects the city with other charming destinations in Spain. Consider taking a scenic train journey to experience the beauty of the Spanish countryside and discover the allure of nearby towns.

10. Sky-High Splendour: Cable Car to Monte

Ascend to new heights with a cable car ride to Monte, providing breathtaking views of Santander and its surroundings. This elevated journey adds a touch of aerial splendour to your transportation repertoire.

11. Cruise Control: Rental Boats for Bay Exploration

Santander's Bay is a maritime playground, and renting a boat allows you to explore its tranquil waters at your own pace. Cruise along the coastline, anchor in secluded coves, and indulge in a nautical adventure.

12. Airport Alacrity: Santander Airport Connections

For air travellers, Santander Airport provides convenient connections to and from the city. Whether arriving or departing, transportation to the airport is readily available, ensuring a smooth transition between air and land.

13. Tuk-Tuk Tales: Quirky City Tours

Dive into a unique experience by exploring the city in a tuk-tuk. These quirky vehicles offer guided tours, weaving through Santander's streets while providing entertaining insights into its history and culture.

Santander's transportation options form a diverse tapestry, offering travellers the freedom to choose their own mode of exploration. Whether you're strolling along the coastline, cruising on a ferry, or embarking on a train journey, each mode of transportation contributes to the city's unique charm. So, embrace the transportation odyssey, and let Santander's enchanting avenues unfold before you. Safe travels!

Safety and Security

Nurturing Serenity: A Guide to Safety and Security in Santander

Santander, with its coastal allure and cultural treasures, offers a haven of tranquillity for travellers. While the city embraces visitors with open arms, ensuring your safety and security is of paramount importance. Here's a guide to fostering serenity during your sojourn in Santander:

1. Coastal Vigilance

Santander's waterfront is a picturesque gem, but like any coastal city, it's essential to be aware of your surroundings. Enjoy the scenic beauty but keep a vigilant eye on your belongings, especially in bustling areas and popular tourist spots.

2. Stroll with Confidence

The heart of Santander invites leisurely strolls through its charming streets. Feel free to wander, but be confident and purposeful in your movements. Projecting assurance can deter unwanted attention.

3. Light-Footed Evenings

Santander's evenings are enchanting, and exploring the city after dark can be a magical experience. Stick to well-lit areas, especially when venturing into neighbourhoods or parks during night-time hours.

4. Pocketing Possessions

Keep your belongings secure by using anti-theft measures, such as cross-body bags or money belts. Be mindful of pickpockets in crowded places and avoid displaying valuables unnecessarily.

5. Technological Vigilance

Be cautious with your electronic devices. Keep an eye on your Smartphone, camera, and other gadgets, especially in outdoor settings where they might be more vulnerable.

6. Know Your Emergency Contacts

Familiarise yourself with local emergency numbers and the location of the nearest embassy or consulate. Having this information at hand provides a sense of security in case of unexpected situations.

7. Travel with Group Gusto

Travelling with a group, especially during night-time excursions, adds an extra layer of security. Enjoy the city's nightlife with friends or fellow travellers to share the enchantment and look out for each other.

8. Trustworthy Transits

When using public transportation or taxis, opt for reputable providers. Official taxis have clear signage, and public transportation services are well-regulated, providing a secure means of getting around the city.

9. Hotel Homestead

Choose accommodations wisely. Opt for reputable hotels or accommodations with positive reviews. Most establishments prioritise guest safety, and their local insights can enhance your overall security.

10. Connect with Locals

Engage with locals to gather insights on safe places to explore and receive valuable tips. Locals often provide a genuine perspective on navigating the city and avoiding any potential pitfalls.

11. Cultural Sensitivity

Respect local customs and traditions. Being culturally sensitive fosters positive interactions and contributes to a harmonious experience. Santander's residents appreciate visitors who embrace their cultural nuances.

12. Beachside Awareness

If you're enjoying Santander's beaches, keep an eye on the tides, especially if you decide to take a dip. Beach safety is crucial, so adhere to any warnings or guidelines provided by lifeguards.

13. Street Smart Dining

Savour the local cuisine in Santander's charming eateries. Choose well-established restaurants and street food vendors with good hygiene practices to ensure a delightful and safe culinary experience.

14. Navigate Nightlife Wisely

While Santander's nightlife is vibrant and inviting, exercise caution and moderation. Be aware of your surroundings, trust your instincts, and choose reputable venues for a night of celebration.

15. Report and Seek Assistance

In the rare event of an incident, don't hesitate to report it to local authorities. Santander prioritises the safety of its residents and visitors, and seeking assistance ensures a prompt and effective response.

Santander, with its coastal grace and welcoming atmosphere, is a city that prioritises the well-being of its visitors. By embracing these safety and security guidelines, you pave the way for a serene and unforgettable exploration of this enchanting Spanish gem. So, immerse yourself in the cultural tapestry, savour the coastal vistas, and relish every moment of your Santander adventure. Safe travels!

Language Symphony

Language Symphony: Navigating Santander's Conversational Seas

Embarking on a linguistic journey through Santander is akin to delving into a symphony of expressions. Spanish is the melody that resonates through the city's streets, creating a harmonious atmosphere for communication. Here's a guide to navigating Santander's conversational seas and enhancing your cultural immersion.

1. Embrace the Melody of Spanish

Spanish is the soulful melody of Santander. While many locals may understand English, embracing basic Spanish phrases adds a delightful note to your interactions. A simple "Hola" (Hello) or "Gracias" (Thank you) can open doors and hearts.

2. Sprinkle Courtesy Phrases

Infuse your conversations with courtesy phrases like "Porfavor" (Please) and "Perdón" (Excuse me). These gestures of politeness are appreciated and contribute to the warmth of your interactions.

3. Dive into Culinary Conversations

When exploring Santander's culinary scene, knowing a few food-related terms can elevate your dining experience. "Menú del día" refers to the daily menu, and "Vino tinto" is red wine, adding flavourful nuances to your gastronomic journey.

4. Navigate Numerical Waters

Familiarise yourself with numerical expressions to effortlessly navigate transactions and directions. Numbers like "uno" to "diez" (one to ten) and basic counting can prove invaluable when making purchases or asking for quantities.

5. Appreciate Local Accents

Santander may have its unique regional accents and colloquial expressions. Embrace these nuances with curiosity, and locals will likely appreciate your interest in the intricacies of their language.

6. Engage in Charismatic Greetings

Greetings are the overture to meaningful interactions. "Buenos días" (Good morning), "Buenas tardes" (Good afternoon), and "Buenas noches" (Good night) are the charismatic notes that set the tone for friendly exchanges.

7. Language of Art and Culture

Santander's art and cultural spaces may have bilingual signage, but a basic understanding of terms like "arte" (art), "historia" (history), and "cultura" (culture) can enhance your appreciation during museum visits and cultural explorations.

8. Navigate the Mercado Dialogue

Exploring markets like Mercado de la Esperanza is a feast for the senses. Familiarise yourself with terms like "frutas" (fruits), "verduras" (vegetables), and "queso" (cheese) to engage in delightful conversations with local vendors.

9. Ask for Recommendations

Don't hesitate to ask for recommendations using phrases like "Qué recomienda?" (What do you recommend?) when seeking advice from locals. This not only enhances your experience but also fosters engaging conversations.

10. Explore Language Learning Apps

Consider using language learning apps to brush up on essential phrases before and during your trip. Apps like Duolingo or Babbel can add an interactive dimension to your linguistic journey.

11. Celebrate Festivals with Expressions

Santander's festivals are vibrant celebrations of culture. Learning expressions like "Feliz Navidad!" (Merry Christmas) or "Felices Fiestas!" (Happy Holidays) allows you to join in the festive cheer during special occasions.

12. Exchange Cultural Insights

Engage in conversations about Santander's rich cultural tapestry. Expressing interest in local customs and traditions with phrases like "Cuéntame más sobre..." (Tell me more about...) invites locals to share their cultural insights.

13. Grasp Transportation Terms

Understanding transportation terms enhances your mobility. Phrases like "Estación de tren" (Train station) and "Parada de autobús" (Bus stop) ensure smooth interactions when navigating Santander's transportation network.

14. Language Exchange Enthusiasm

Santander residents often appreciate language exchange. If you're keen on practising Spanish, express your interest with phrases like "Podemos practicar español?" (Can we practise Spanish?), creating an opportunity for cultural exchange.

15. Immerse in Local Stories

Dive into local stories by engaging with residents in places like cafés or local hangouts. Phrases like "Cuéntame Más Sobre Este Lugar?" (Tell me more about this place?) Can unveil hidden narratives and enrich your Santander experience.

Santander's linguistic tapestry is woven with the threads of warmth and hospitality. By embracing the language symphony, you not only navigate the city with ease but also open doors to authentic connections and cultural revelations. So, let the language of Santander serenade your senses, and may your conversations be as enchanting as the city itself! Buena suerte! (Good luck!)

CHAPTER TEN

Santander in Every Season

Santander's Ever-Changing Canvas: A Seasonal Symphony

Santander, like a versatile artist, unveils its beauty in a seasonal symphony, each movement painting the city with unique hues and atmospheres. Whether you find yourself under the warm embrace of summer or the subtle chill of winter, Santander's charm remains ever-present, offering a diverse palette of experiences to enchant your senses.

Spring

Santander's Springtime Sonata: Nature's Reawakening

In Santander, spring unfolds like a sonata, a harmonious melody that transforms the city into a canvas of vibrant colours and delicate fragrances. As winter's embrace loosens, Santander's landscapes burst forth in a celebration of renewal, inviting residents and visitors alike to immerse themselves in the enchanting symphony of spring.

1. Floral Flourish in Parks

Santander's parks, like Jardines de Piquio and the Magdalena Peninsula, awaken with a floral flourish in spring. Blossoming cherry blossoms, vibrant tulips, and fragrant magnolias transform these green oases into a kaleidoscope of colours, creating a captivating backdrop for leisurely strolls.

2. Coastal Blooms Along Promenades

The city's coastal promenades come alive with blooming flowers, adding a touch of romance to seaside walks. As you stroll along El Sardinero beach, the gentle sea breeze carries the sweet scent of spring blooms, creating an immersive experience that captivates the senses.

3. Garden of Magdalena Palace Awakens

The gardens surrounding the Magdalena Palace, a regal residence overlooking the bay, awaken from their winter slumber. Magnificent roses, daffodils, and azaleas paint a vibrant tableau, inviting visitors to wander through this horticultural paradise overlooking the shimmering waters of the Bay of Santander.

4. Seaside Cafés Bursting with Life

Santander's seaside cafés, already charming, come alive in spring. Terrace tables adorned with colourful flowers create inviting spaces where patrons can bask in the sunshine. Savouring a cup of coffee or a refreshing beverage becomes a sensory delight amidst the blossoming coastal ambiance.

5. Beachside Bliss and Maritime Magic

El Sardinero beach becomes a haven for sun-seekers, and the sound of waves accompanies the joyous laughter of beachgoers. Spring marks the beginning of beachside bliss, where sands become a canvas for sunbathing and enjoying the maritime magic that defines Santander's coastal allure.

6. Botanical Symphony in Greenhouses

Santander's botanical gardens come alive with a botanical symphony as exotic plants and tropical flowers unfurl their petals. Greenhouses become sanctuaries of biodiversity, allowing visitors to embark on a journey through the world's flora without leaving the city.

7. Exploring Coastal Walkways

Coastal walkways, like the one leading to Faro de Cabo Mayor, beckon adventurers to explore their scenic beauty. Lush greenery lines the paths, and the cliffs offer panoramic views of the Bay of Santander, creating an idyllic setting for those seeking a springtime adventure.

8. Cultural Events Blossom

Spring in Santander is not only a celebration of nature but also a blossoming of cultural events. Open-air concerts, art exhibitions, and street performances add a cultural flair to the season, turning the city into a vibrant stage for artistic expression.

9. Blooms Adorning Historic Architecture

Santander's historic architecture, from the Cathedral to the University of Cantabria, is adorned with blossoms in spring. Wisteria-covered facades and flower-filled balconies contribute to the city's aesthetic charm, creating a captivating interplay between history and nature.

10. Seasonal Delicacies at Markets

Spring brings an abundance of seasonal delicacies to Santander's markets. Fresh fruits, early vegetables, and artisanal products fill the stalls, inviting locals and visitors to indulge in the flavours of the season and embark on a culinary journey through springtime delights.

11. Tranquil Reflections in Gardens

Santander's gardens, such as the Parque de las Llamas, offer tranquil reflections in spring. Ponds adorned with water lilies, vibrant meadows, and the gentle hum of bees create a serene atmosphere, providing a peaceful escape for those seeking moments of introspection.

12. Nautical Adventures in Milder Climes

With milder temperatures, spring becomes an ideal time for nautical adventures. Boat trips across the Bay of Santander reveal the city's coastal beauty from a different perspective, allowing passengers to witness the maritime symphony of waves and seagulls.

13. Spring Festivals and Traditions

Santander's springtime calendar is marked by festivals and traditions that bring communities together. Whether it's the celebration of Semana Santa (Holy Week) or local festivities, spring becomes a time for communal joy, traditional music, and colourful processions.

14. Vibrant Street Markets

Spring sees the emergence of vibrant street markets throughout Santander. Mercado de la Esperanza, in particular, becomes a hub of activity, with stalls offering fresh produce, handmade crafts, and local treats, creating a lively atmosphere that mirrors the season's vitality.

15. Blossoming Romance in Every Corner

Romance blossoms in every corner of Santander during spring. From secret gardens to intimate cafés, the city becomes a backdrop for shared moments, blooming love stories, and the promise of new beginnings in the warm embrace of the season.

Santander's springtime sonata is a symphony of renewal, where nature and culture intertwine to create an enchanting experience for all who wander through its blossoming streets. As the city emerges from winter's embrace, Santander invites you to join in the celebration of life's resurgence and embrace the beauty that unfolds with each petal and note of the springtime melody. Bienvenido a la primavera! (Welcome to spring!)

Summer

Santander's Summer Symphony: A Coastal Overture

As the sun ascends to its zenith, Santander transforms into a coastal symphony during the radiant days of summer. The city, kissed by the warmth of the sun and caressed by sea breezes, becomes a vibrant stage where residents and visitors alike revel in the joyful crescendo of seasonal delights. Here's a poetic ode to Santander's summer enchantment.

1. Sunlit Serenity on El Sardinero Beach

El Sardinero, with its golden sands stretching under the caress of the sun, becomes a haven of sunlit serenity. The rhythmic lull of the waves accompanies the laughter of beachgoers, creating a timeless tableau of coastal bliss.

2. Coastal Cafés and Seaside Sips

Seaside cafés, their terraces adorned with colourful umbrellas, beckon patrons to savour the essence of summer. Sipping on cooling beverages, whether it's a refreshing tinto de verano or an iced coffee, becomes a sensory delight against the backdrop of the glistening sea.

3. Maritime Adventures

The Bay of Santander, dotted with sailboats and kayaks, becomes a playground for maritime adventures. Whether you're setting sail to explore the coast or paddling along tranquil waters, the maritime symphony of summer unfolds as an invitation to embrace the sea.

4. Festive Nights and Beachside Soirées

Summer nights in Santander are a tapestry of festive lights and beachside soirées. El Sardinero comes alive with music, dance, and the cheerful chatter of locals and visitors mingling in the warm evening air, creating an ambiance of spirited celebration.

5. Sunset Strolls on the Promenade

The waterfront promenades, kissed by the hues of the setting sun, become a canvas for romantic sunset strolls. Couples saunter hand in hand, basking in the golden glow that transforms the Bay of Santander into a breathtaking panorama.

6. Culinary Delights with Ocean Views

Dining in Santander reaches new heights during summer, with ocean-view restaurants offering culinary delights infused with seasonal freshness. Seafood feasts, accompanied by local wines, become a gastronomic journey that mirrors the abundance of the sea.

7. Artistic Expression Under Open Skies

Summer invites artistic expression under open skies. Street performers, musicians, and artists grace the city's squares and waterfront, adding a creative flair to Santander's vibrant summer streets.

8. Hidden Coves and Coastal Retreats

Beyond the bustling beaches, hidden coves and coastal retreats unveil themselves. Exploring these serene corners becomes a summer adventure, where tranquillity reigns, and the turquoise waters beckon for a secluded dip.

9. Nautical Elegance of Regattas

Santander's nautical elegance takes centre stage with summer regattas. Sailboats, their sails billowing in the breeze, participate in maritime spectacles that unfold against the backdrop of the city's historic architecture and scenic coastline.

10. Vibrant Nightlife in Plaza Cañadío

Plaza Cañadío, a lively square in the city centre, becomes a hub of vibrant nightlife. Bars and terraces overflow with patrons enjoying tapas, laughter, and live music, creating an atmosphere where the spirit of summer revelry is alive and contagious.

11. Coastal Walkways Illuminated by Moonlight

Coastal walkways, illuminated by the soft glow of moonlight, invite enchanting nocturnal walks. The sea's gentle whispers intertwine with the laughter of those strolling along the promenade, creating a serene and magical ambiance.

12. Maritime Markets and Seaside Treasures

Summer markets along the waterfront become treasure troves of maritime delights. From handmade crafts to fresh catches of the day, these markets offer a glimpse into Santander's coastal heritage and provide an opportunity to savour local flavours.

13. Beach Volleyball and Sandy Playgrounds

El Sardinero transforms into a sandy playground where beach volleyball matches unfold against the backdrop of the sea. The laughter of friends engaged in spirited games becomes a joyful soundtrack to the summer days.

14. Picnics in Parque de las Llamas

Parque de las Llamas, a verdant oasis in the heart of the city, becomes a perfect setting for summer picnics. Families and friends gather under the shade of lush trees, indulging in culinary delights amidst the greenery.

15. Majestic Views from Faro de Cabo Mayor

Faro de Cabo Mayor, perched on the cliffs overlooking the Bay of Santander, becomes a vantage point for majestic views. Watching the sunset from this iconic lighthouse becomes a summer ritual, where the horizon meets the sea in a blaze of colours.

Santander's summer symphony is a celebration of life, where the city's coastal spirit harmonises with the vibrant energy of the season. Whether you're savouring culinary delights, engaging in maritime adventures, or simply basking in the warmth of the sun, Santander invites you to dance to the rhythm of its summer enchantment. Viva el verano! (Long live summer!)

Autumn

Santander's Autumnal Sonata: A Symphony of Amber Hues

As the sun gracefully begins its descent and the air adopts a gentle crispness, Santander embraces a melodic transformation, painting the city in a palette of warm and inviting autumnal hues. The coastal breeze carries with it a sense of reflection, turning the city into a symphony of amber tones and nostalgic melodies. Here's an expressive journey through Santander's autumnal serenade.

1. Rustic Charm Along Coastal Promenades

The coastal promenades, kissed by the autumn sun, don a rustic charm. Trees adorned in shades of amber and gold line the waterfront, creating a picturesque setting for contemplative strolls against the backdrop of the Bay of Santander.

2. Romantic Sunsets Over the Sea

Autumn sunsets in Santander become a romantic spectacle. The sun bids farewell to the day, casting a warm glow over El Sardinero beach. Couples gather to witness the amber and pink hues reflecting on the tranquil waters, creating a mesmerising display of nature's artistry.

3. Maritime Magic in Crisp Air

The crisp autumn air brings a touch of magic to Santander's maritime ambiance. Sailboats gracefully navigate the bay, their white sails contrasting against the deep blue sea and the amber tones of the changing leaves along the coastline.

4. Tranquil Moments in Hidden Gardens

Hidden gardens, such as those within the Magdalena Peninsula, become havens of tranquillity. The crunch of fallen leaves underfoot accompanies quiet moments of reflection amidst the changing foliage, creating a serene escape from the everyday hustle.

5. Cosy Cafés and Steaming Beverages

Cosy cafés along the streets of Santander offer refuge from the autumn chill. Steaming cups of coffee, cocoa, or tea become companions for those seeking warmth, and the aroma of seasonal spices fills the air, inviting patrons to linger in the comfort of these charming spaces.

6. Fading Sunlight on Historical Architecture

The historical architecture of Santander, from the Cathedral to the Magdalena Palace, is bathed in the soft glow of fading sunlight. The amber hues cast shadows that accentuate the intricate details of these structures, creating a visual tapestry that reflects the city's rich history.

7. Seaside Markets with Autumnal Harvest

Seaside markets, like Mercado de la Esperanza, showcase an autumnal harvest of fresh produce. Pumpkins, apples, and chestnuts fill the stalls, inviting locals and visitors to savour the flavours of the season and embark on a culinary journey through autumn's bounty.

8. Maritime Walkways Adorned in Autumnal Beauty

Santander's maritime walkways, such as those leading to Faro de Cabo Mayor, are adorned in autumnal beauty. Trees and shrubs transform into fiery hues, creating a vibrant corridor where the gentle sea breeze carries the scent of saltwater mingled with the earthy fragrance of fallen leaves.

9. Intimate Evenings in Seaside Cafés

Seaside cafés take on an intimate ambiance during autumn evenings. Dimmed lights and the gentle murmur of the sea create a romantic setting for shared moments, where patrons can savour both the coastal beauty and the warmth of companionship.

10. Cultural Venues Illuminated by Autumn Moonlight

Cultural venues, whether museums or historic sites, are illuminated by the soft glow of autumn moonlight. Night-time visits to these places become a magical experience, where history and art intertwine under the enchanting embrace of the season.

11. Autumnal Adventures to Nearby Villages

Autumn becomes an ideal time for day trips to nearby villages, where the countryside is ablaze with the hues of fall. Exploring quaint locales like Somo or Comillas offers a glimpse into rural life, complete with charming landscapes and cosy cafés.

12. Harvest Festivals and Traditional Celebrations

Santander's autumn calendar is marked by harvest festivals and traditional celebrations. Whether it's a local fair or a cultural event, these gatherings bring communities together, creating an atmosphere of shared joy and communal spirit.

13. Windswept Beach Walks and Contemplation

Windswept beach walks become a contemplative activity during autumn. The symphony of crashing waves and the rustle of leaves on the sand create a soothing backdrop for introspection, inviting individuals to connect with nature in its quieter moments.

14. Hidden Coastal Retreats in Autumn Silence

Hidden coastal retreats, away from the bustling beaches, offer solace in the autumn silence. Secluded corners become havens for those seeking moments of serenity, where the sound of the sea and the rustling leaves create a harmonious melody.

15. Autumnal Aromas in Local Markets

Local markets, such as Mercado de la Esperanza, are filled with autumnal aromas. Spices, roasted chestnuts, and seasonal treats create a sensory experience, enticing visitors to indulge in the scents and flavours that define Santander's autumnal charm.

Santander's autumnal sonata is a symphony of transition, where the city gracefully embraces the changing season. Each rustle of leaves, each fading sunset, and each sip of steaming beverage become notes in this seasonal composition, inviting residents and visitors to savour the beauty that unfolds in the amber embrace of autumn. Bienvenido al otoño! (Welcome to autumn!)

Winter

Santander's Winter Elegance: A Frosty Poem

In the heart of winter, Santander dons an elegant cloak of frost, transforming into a city of enchanting stillness. The air, crisp and invigorating, carries with it the hushed whispers of the season. Amidst historic architecture and along the coastal promenades, Santander unveils its winter elegance, a poetic dance with nature's icy grace.

1. Coastal Silence and Icy Breezes

Along the coastal promenades, a gentle hush descends with the arrival of winter. Icy breezes from the Bay of Santander weave through the air, creating a symphony of silence that harmonises with the rhythmic lull of the sea.

2. Timeless Beauty of Historic Architecture

Historic architecture, such as the Magdalena Palace and the Cathedral, stands as timeless sentinels in the winter landscape. Adorned with a delicate dusting of frost, these structures exude an ethereal beauty that transports visitors to a bygone era.

3. Cosy **Cafés and Steamed Windows**

Cosy cafés, their windows steamed with the warmth within, become sanctuaries from the winter chill. Patrons, wrapped in scarves and sipping hot beverages, create an intimate tableau against the backdrop of the city's frost-kissed streets.

4. Maritime Serenity Under Winter Skies

The Bay of Santander, under winter skies, becomes a canvas of serenity. Seagulls soar above the frosty waters, and the distant sound of waves against the shore creates a soothing melody, inviting contemplation and quiet admiration.

5. Luminous Nights Along El Sardinero

El Sardinero, aglow with winter lights, transforms into a luminous spectacle. Evening strolls along the beachfront reveal a magical world of twinkling lights, creating a whimsical ambiance that contrasts with the crisp darkness of winter nights.

6. Cultural Venues Illuminated by Festive Lights

Cultural venues, adorned with festive lights, add a touch of magic to winter nights. Museums and historic sites, such as the Botín Centre, become beacons of cultural illumination, inviting visitors to explore their treasures under the enchanting glow.

7. Maritime Adventures in Winter Calm

Winter's calm invites maritime adventures, where sailboats gently navigate the still waters of the Bay of Santander. Against a backdrop of frost-kissed cliffs, these seafaring vessels create a scene of quiet elegance, blending with the winter serenity.

8. Quaint Markets with Seasonal Delights

Quaint markets, like Mercado de la Esperanza, brim with seasonal delights. Stalls offer winter fruits, artisanal treats, and festive decorations, creating a market scene where the aromas of the season mingle with the joyful chatter of visitors.

9. Cosy Evenings in Historic Pubs

Historic pubs, their interiors aglow with warm hues, beckon for cosy evenings. Patrons gather around crackling fireplaces, sharing stories and savouring hearty fare, creating a scene of camaraderie amidst the winter chill.

10. Maritime Muse at Faro de Cabo Mayor

Faro de Cabo Mayor, perched on the frosty cliffs, becomes a maritime muse under winter skies. The sweeping views of the Bay of Santander and the distant horizon create a breathtaking panorama, where the sea meets the frost-kissed landscape.

11. Winter Walks in Hidden Gardens

Hidden gardens, such as those within the Magdalena Peninsula, invite winter walks amidst their serene landscapes. Frost-kissed foliage and icy ponds reflect the seasonal beauty, providing a tranquil escape within the city.

12. Christmas Markets and Festive Cheer

Christmas markets infuse Santander with festive cheer. The Plaza Porticada, adorned with twinkling lights, becomes a hub of holiday spirit. Market stalls offer handmade crafts, seasonal treats, and a joyful atmosphere that defines winter in the city.

13. Windswept Beaches and Contemplation

Windswept beaches, adorned with a delicate layer of frost, invite contemplative walks. The sound of the waves against the frozen sands creates a poetic backdrop, where the beauty of winter unfolds in the simplicity of nature.

14. Winter Sunsets over El Sardinero

Winter sunsets over El Sardinero cast a breathtaking palette of colours. The sky becomes a canvas of pinks, purples, and oranges, reflecting on the frost-kissed waters and creating a mesmerising spectacle that marks the end of the winter day.

15. Culinary Delights in Cosy Taverns

Cosy taverns, with their rustic charm, offer culinary delights that warm the soul. From hearty stews to seasonal desserts, these establishments become havens for those seeking the comforting flavours of winter against the backdrop of Santander's historic charm.

Santander's winter elegance is a poetic interlude, where the city's beauty intertwines with the serene grace of the season. Each frost-kissed moment, from maritime adventures to cosy evenings, becomes a verse in the winter symphony that invites residents and visitors to savour the quiet splendour of this frosty embrace. Bienvenido al invierno! (Welcome to winter!)

CHAPTER ELEVEN

Glossary of Local Terms

1. Sobremesa

Definition: A cherished Spanish tradition, sobremesa refers to the leisurely time spent at the table after a meal, engaging in conversation, savouring coffee or dessert. Embrace this cultural ritual to truly appreciate the art of lingering over good company.

2. Terruño

Definition: Literally translating to "homeland" or "place of origin," terruño encapsulates the deep connection Santanderinos have with their roots and the sense of pride associated with their local identity.

3. Poteo

Definition: The practice of going from one bar to another, enjoying small dishes or tapas at each stop. Poteo captures the essence of socialising and sampling diverse culinary delights in the company of friends.

4. Cantábrico

Definition: Referring to the Cantabrian Sea, which bathes the shores of Santander. Locals use this term with a sense of reverence, acknowledging the sea's influence on the city's climate, cuisine, and way of life.

5. Recaero

Definition: A local term for someone who enjoys spending time outdoors, particularly in parks, plazas, or along the picturesque waterfront. Santander's beautiful natural spaces attract many recaeros seeking tranquillity and fresh air.

6. Despacho

Definition: Beyond its literal meaning of "office," despacho is a colloquial term for a bar or café. It's a place where locals gather to socialise, unwind, and enjoy a cup of coffee or a refreshing beverage.

7. Sardinero

Definition: Named after the district, El Sardinero, this term has become synonymous with the city's famous beaches. When locals refer to "going to Sardinero," they are likely headed to enjoy the sun, sand, and lively atmosphere by the sea.

8. Chufa

Definition: While it may sound exotic, chufa refers to tiger nuts, often used in the preparation of horchata, a refreshing drink popular during the warmer months. Embrace the local flavours by trying chufa-based beverages.

9. Amagüestu

Definition: A celebration of the Asturian tradition where locals gather for a communal feast featuring chestnuts and cider. In Santander, you may encounter amagüestu-inspired events during the autumn season.

10. Güevos Pintos

Definition: Literally meaning "painted eggs," güevos pintos refer to a traditional dish involving boiled eggs adorned with colourful designs. It's often enjoyed during Easter celebrations, adding a festive touch to local gatherings.

11. Bocata

Definition: A casual and beloved term for a sandwich or a snack. Whether filled with local cheeses, cured meats, or fresh seafood, indulging in a bocata is a delicious way to experience Santander's culinary diversity.

12. Rastro

Definition: Translating to "trail" or "trace," rastro is commonly used to refer to flea markets or second-hand markets. Explore the local rastro to uncover unique treasures and vintage finds.

13. Atracón

Definition: Describing a hearty and satisfying meal, atracón captures the essence of indulging in a feast or a substantial culinary experience. It's an invitation to savour every bite and embrace the pleasure of good food.

14. Verbena

Definition: A festive celebration often accompanied by music, dancing, and merriment. Santander's verbenas, held during special occasions, offer a lively atmosphere where locals and visitors come together to enjoy the rhythm of traditional music.

15. Campero

Definition: Typically referring to a light and informal meal, often enjoyed outdoors or on the go. A campero might involve sandwiches, salads, or other casual fare perfect for a picnic in one of Santander's scenic spots.

16. Bolera

Definition: Originating from the traditional game of bowling, bolera is also used to describe a local venue or gathering place. Whether it's a bowling alley or a social hotspot, boleras are synonymous with leisure and camaraderie.

17. Aguinaldo

Definition: A gift or a token of appreciation often exchanged during festive seasons or special occasions. Experiencing aguinaldo reflects the warmth and generosity ingrained in Santander's cultural celebrations.

18. Romería

Definition: A religious pilgrimage or procession, often involving a journey to a sacred site or shrine. Santander's romerías are vibrant events, combining religious devotion with joyful festivities and communal gatherings.

19. Trozo

Definition: A slice or portion, frequently used when referring to a piece of cake, pie, or any delectable treat. Indulge in the diverse trozos offered by Santander's patisseries and dessert spots.

20. Sobao

Definition: A traditional Cantabrian sponge cake, known for its rich flavour and moist texture. Sampling a sobao is a delightful way to savour a sweet piece of Santander's culinary heritage.

By incorporating these local terms into your conversations and experiences, you'll not only navigate Santander's cultural nuances with ease but also connect more deeply with the spirit of the city. Que disfrutes de tu aventura! (Enjoy your adventure!)

Printed in Great Britain
by Amazon

41563659R00175